RSI Trading Mastery: Strategies with the Relative Strength Index for Consistent Profits

Master the Relative Strength Index and transform market noise into consistent opportunity

By Grant Westbrook

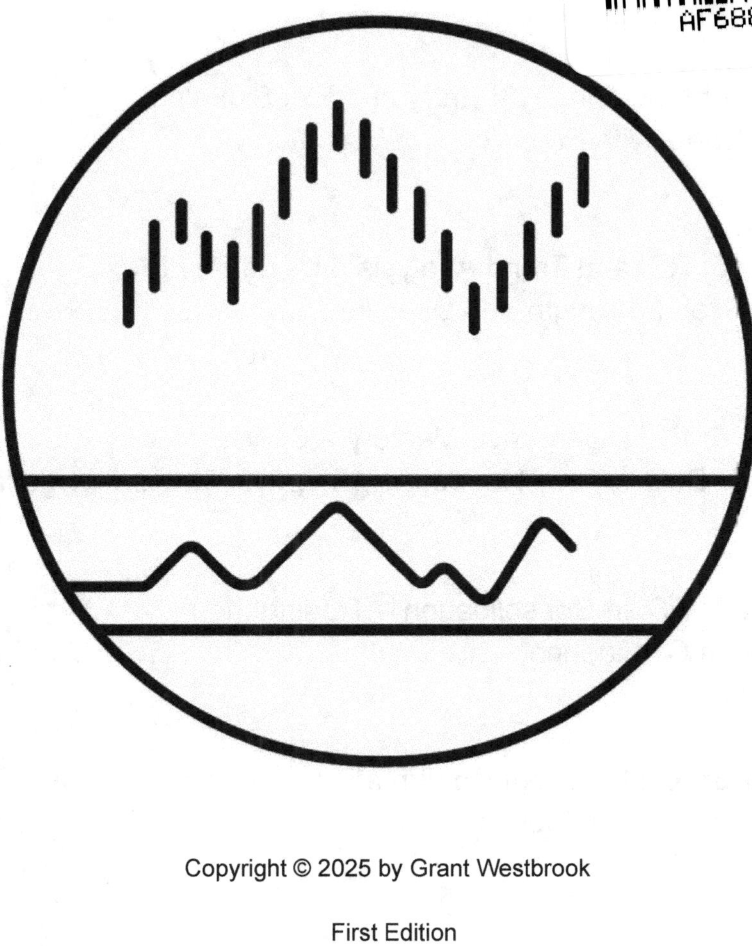

First Edition

Table of Contents

Introduction

Mastering the markets doesn't require a dozen indicators, endless chart clutter, or guesswork. In fact, one of the most powerful tools in technical analysis has been hiding in plain sight on trading platforms for decades—**the Relative Strength Index**, or **RSI**.

Whether you're a beginner trying to understand when to enter a trade, or an experienced trader looking to refine your edge, this book will equip you with the **complete playbook for using RSI** like the pros do. While many traders use RSI only as an "overbought or oversold" gauge, the truth is that **RSI is a multi-dimensional indicator** capable of:

- Spotting high-probability reversals
- Confirming the strength of trends
- Identifying hidden market divergence
- Acting as a precise entry and exit tool when combined with price structure

The RSI, developed by J. Welles Wilder Jr., is a **momentum oscillator**—but it's far more than just a number that bounces between 0 and 100. It tells a story. And if you learn to read it correctly, that story can mean the difference between a missed opportunity and a perfectly timed, high-reward trade.

This guide is designed to be **the only RSI book you'll ever need**. You'll go beyond surface-level definitions and uncover how RSI truly works under the hood. We'll explore how to:

- Interpret RSI in real-time market environments
- Avoid common RSI misuses that lead to losses
- Customize RSI to fit your personal strategy
- Combine RSI with other tools for maximum edge

We'll walk through clear examples, step-by-step strategies, and battle-tested techniques for using RSI across different markets—including **stocks, futures, crypto, and forex**. And by the end, you'll have a complete, professional-grade understanding of RSI and how to use it as a cornerstone in your trading system.

What You'll Gain from This Book

- Clarity: No fluff, no filler—just straight-up actionable RSI education.
- Confidence: You'll know **when to act**, **why you're acting**, and **what to expect**.
- Consistency: RSI will become a **repeatable tool** in your strategy arsenal—backed by logic, not luck.

Let's move beyond theory. Let's make RSI work for you.

Let's begin.

Chapter 1

Understanding RSI – The Core Concepts

Introduction

The Relative Strength Index (RSI) is one of the most popular and powerful tools in a trader's arsenal. Developed by J. Welles Wilder in 1978, RSI is a momentum oscillator that measures the speed and change of price movements. Despite its simplicity, this single indicator can help you identify potential reversals, confirm trends, and time high-probability trades across all markets and timeframes.

Whether you're day trading oil futures, swing trading tech stocks, or scalping crypto, RSI gives you a real-time window into the strength of price action—and when that strength might be about to shift.

What Does RSI Actually Measure?

- RSI quantifies **momentum** by comparing the magnitude of recent gains to recent losses over a specified time period—usually 14 periods.

- The resulting value oscillates between **0 and 100**. It doesn't show price, but rather **the rate at which price is moving**—a subtle but powerful distinction.

- A **high RSI** suggests strong recent gains, possibly indicating an overbought condition.

- A **low RSI** reflects recent selling pressure, often signaling an oversold market.

This dynamic view of strength vs weakness allows RSI to anticipate potential shifts in trend before price itself shows a clear reversal.

How Is RSI Calculated?

Understanding the math behind RSI gives you confidence and clarity when using it in live markets. Here's a simplified breakdown:

- RSI = 100 - [100 / (1 + RS)]
- RS = Average Gain over X periods / Average Loss over X periods
- Default X = 14 periods (you can customize this)

Example:

- Let's say over 14 periods, the average gain was 1.2 and the average loss was 0.6.
- RS = 1.2 / 0.6 = 2
- RSI = 100 - [100 / (1 + 2)] = 100 - [100 / 3] = 66.67

This would indicate a moderately strong uptrend—getting close to "overbought" levels, but not extreme.

The Overbought/Oversold Framework

- **Overbought** typically refers to RSI values above **70**
- **Oversold** is generally marked by RSI values below **30**
- These are **not automatic reversal zones**, but potential warning signs that a reversal or pullback could be near
- For more aggressive setups, some traders use 80/20 as extreme overbought/oversold markers, especially in fast-moving markets like futures or crypto

The key takeaway is that RSI doesn't tell you when to enter—it tells you **when to start paying close attention**.

Example:

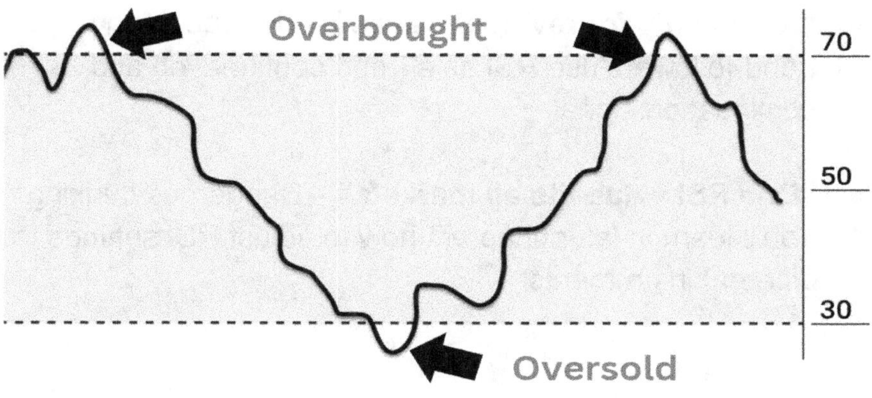

Illustration of overbought & oversold levels of the RSI indicator

RSI's Strength as a Leading Indicator

- RSI is **not lagging** like moving averages—it can often **lead price**, especially during divergence setups
- This makes RSI ideal for traders seeking **early warning signs** of exhaustion or momentum reversals
- It shines in both **range-bound environments** (as a reversal tool) and in **trending markets** (as a momentum filter)

Common Misunderstandings About RSI

- **“Overbought means it has to go down”** – False. In strong trends, RSI can stay overbought/oversold for extended periods.
- **“RSI is only for reversal trades”** – Not true. Many trend-followers use RSI as a trend confirmation and continuation signal.
- **“One RSI value fits all markets”** – Dangerous thinking. You’ll learn in later chapters how to adjust RSI settings to fit different instruments.

RSI Works Across All Markets

- **Futures (e.g. CL, ES, GC):** Use RSI for timing mean reversion and divergence trades intraday
- **Stocks & ETFs:** Use RSI to confirm pullbacks in trending stocks or find exhausted breakout attempts
- **Crypto:** RSI helps in navigating volatility by highlighting emotional extremes
- **Forex:** In range-heavy markets like EUR/USD, RSI excels at finding bounce zones

Summary

RSI is a versatile, momentum-based oscillator that helps traders identify potential turning points and confirm the strength of price action. Its simplicity hides a deep well of strategic applications—from scalping reversals in oil futures to confirming swing trades in stocks. By measuring the relative strength of price over time, RSI becomes a real-time lens into market behavior—allowing traders to stay ahead of the crowd.

Key Takeaways

➤ RSI is a momentum oscillator that ranges between 0 and 100, most often used to identify overbought (>70) and oversold (<30) conditions.

➤ It's calculated by comparing recent average gains to recent average losses over a chosen period, usually 14.

➤ RSI provides early signals of strength/weakness and can be used for both trend continuation and reversal trades.

➤ Common myths—such as RSI being just for reversals or having universal settings—can limit your trading edge.

➤ RSI adapts well to any market, including futures, stocks, forex, and crypto—making it a must-have tool in every trader's toolkit.

Chapter 2

Understanding RSI Settings – Periods, Speeds & Sensitivity

Introduction

The Relative Strength Index (RSI) is not one-size-fits-all. While the standard setting of 14 periods works well for many traders, **understanding how to adjust RSI settings** can help you fine-tune the indicator for different markets, strategies, and timeframes. In this chapter, we'll explore how different period lengths affect the RSI's responsiveness, how to customize it for scalping vs. swing trading, and how to strike a balance between speed and reliability.

What Does the RSI Setting Control?

- The **RSI period** determines how many candles the indicator looks back to calculate its value
- A **shorter period** (e.g., 5 or 7) makes RSI react faster to price changes
- A **longer period** (e.g., 21 or 30) smooths out noise but reacts more slowly
- Think of RSI settings as a **dial between sensitivity and stability**

Standard RSI Setting – Why 14?

- The 14-period RSI was introduced by J. Welles Wilder as the default
- It offers a **balanced view of momentum** without being too reactive
- Most charting platforms default to 14, which adds to its popularity and **self-fulfilling power**
- It works well for general swing trading on **hourly and daily charts** across all futures markets

Fast RSI – Settings of 5 to 9 Periods

- Makes the RSI more **sensitive and responsive to short-term price swings**
- Best for **scalping and intraday strategies**
- Increases the number of overbought/oversold signals
- More prone to **false signals**, so it should be paired with strong confirmation (candles or volume)

Use Cases:

- **Oil futures** – for quick reactions to inventory reports

- **S&P 500 micro futures (MES)** – for 1-minute or 5-minute scalping setups
- **Gold futures** – to catch sharp pullbacks or news-based reversals

Slow RSI – Settings of 20 to 30 Periods

- Produces **fewer, more reliable signals** by smoothing out short-term volatility
- Better for **swing trading and macro setups**
- Reduces whipsaws and false momentum shifts
- Best when paired with a longer trend-following tool like a 50 EMA

Use Cases:

- **Swing trades on gold** using 4H and daily charts
- **Macro trend setups in oil** using weekly charts
- **Position trades in index futures** where timing is less urgent

Choosing RSI Periods Based on Timeframe

- Short timeframes (1m–15m): **RSI 5–9** for quick entries and exits
- Medium timeframes (1H–4H): **RSI 10–14** for balanced entries
- Long timeframes (Daily–Weekly): **RSI 21–30** to focus on high-confidence trades

Aggressive vs. Conservative RSI Settings

Aggressive Settings (Fast RSI):

- More trades, more opportunities
- Increased noise and potential for overtrading
- Works well in **trending markets** with strong momentum

Conservative Settings (Slow RSI):

- Fewer signals, more reliable setups
- Less prone to fakeouts
- Ideal in **choppy or range-bound markets**

Custom RSI Strategy Based on Market Behavior

- Not all markets behave the same—customize RSI to suit their volatility
- **Oil futures:** often require faster RSI (e.g., 9) due to aggressive intraday moves
- **Gold futures:** benefit from smoother RSI (e.g., 14–21) to absorb whipsaws
- **Index futures:** allow flexibility—fast RSI for the open, slow RSI for the close

Tuning RSI Sensitivity for Your Style

- **Scalpers:** use 5–7 RSI + confirmation from candles/volume
- **Day traders:** use 9–14 RSI + multi-timeframe confirmation
- **Swing traders:** use 14–30 RSI + trend filters like moving averages

RSI Speed and Signal Zones

- Faster RSI = wider swings = more time spent in 70/30 zone
- Slower RSI = tighter oscillation = more time around 50 midpoint
- Adjust RSI zones accordingly:
    - Fast RSI: Use 80/20 or even 90/10 zones
    - Slow RSI: Stick with classic 70/30

Summary

Adjusting the RSI settings can completely change how the indicator behaves. Whether you're scalping a volatile crude oil move or holding a swing position on gold, the period you choose will affect how early—or late—you get your signals. By tailoring the RSI to your market, timeframe, and style, you'll get cleaner setups, avoid noise, and execute with greater precision.

Key Takeaways

➤ Shorter RSI periods (5–9) = faster signals, more noise, best for scalping

➤ Standard RSI (14) = balanced performance across most markets

➤ Longer RSI periods (21–30) = smoother, more reliable signals for swing trades

➤ Tailor your RSI based on timeframe, market volatility, and strategy

➤ Fast RSI needs looser overbought/oversold zones (e.g., 80/20), while slower RSI sticks with 70/30

Chapter 3

Setting Up RSI on Popular Trading Platforms

Introduction

Before RSI can be used effectively, you need to set it up correctly on your trading platform. Fortunately, almost every charting platform—free or paid—includes the RSI indicator by default. But to use it like a pro, you must understand the available customization settings, optimal display options, and how to tailor it to your market and strategy.

This chapter will walk you through setting up RSI on the most popular platforms: **TradingView, MetaTrader, Thinkorswim,** and **NinjaTrader,** and show you how to adjust RSI settings to match your trading style.

RSI Setup Basics

- **Default Setting**: Most platforms default to a 14-period RSI.
- **Source**: Typically calculated using the **closing price** of each bar or candle.
- **Overbought/Oversold Levels**: 70/30 levels are usually pre-set.
- **Display Type**: RSI is shown as a **line graph** oscillating between 0–100 in a separate panel below your price chart.

You can customize all of these settings to create a better fit for your asset, timeframe, or trading objective.

Setting Up RSI on TradingView

TradingView is one of the most widely used platforms thanks to its intuitive interface and powerful indicator features.

- Go to your chart and click on **"Indicators"**.
- Search for **"Relative Strength Index"** and click to add it to your chart.
- Customize settings:
    - Click the settings gear icon on the RSI panel.
    - Set **Length** (e.g. 14, 7, 21).
    - Set **Source** (usually "close").
    - Adjust **Upper and Lower Bands** (default: 70 and 30).
- Use **"RSI-based Moving Averages"** for added trend clarity.
- Optionally add background coloring or alert levels to highlight extreme conditions.

TradingView also allows you to **script your own custom RSI** alerts with Pine Script—useful for advanced automation.

Setting Up RSI on MetaTrader 4 & 5

MetaTrader (MT4 and MT5) is widely used for forex and futures trading, especially by algorithmic traders.

- In the **Navigator**, open **Indicators > Oscillators > Relative Strength Index**.
- Drag the indicator onto your chart.
- Adjust settings:
    - **Period** = number of candles (default: 14).
    - Choose a color and line thickness for clarity.
    - Add **horizontal lines at 70 and 30**.
- You can apply RSI to different price types (close, open, high, low) depending on your needs.

MT4 allows for **RSI-based Expert Advisors (EAs)** for automated trading systems.

Setting Up RSI on Thinkorswim (TOS)

Thinkorswim by TD Ameritrade is favored by many U.S. stock and futures traders for its flexibility and speed.

- In the chart window, click on **Studies > Add Study > All Studies > R > RSI**.
- Click the settings icon to customize:
    - **Length** (14 is default, but try 5–7 for short-term scalping).
    - Adjust the overbought/oversold levels from 70/30 to more extreme 80/20 if needed.
- Use RSI **with multiple timeframes** by layering charts or using the "Custom Study" feature.
- TOS also allows you to **create conditional orders** based on RSI values.

This makes RSI integration with your trading strategy seamless and rule-based.

Setting Up RSI on NinjaTrader

NinjaTrader is a futures-focused platform popular for its speed and backtesting tools.

- Right-click on your chart and choose **Indicators**.
- Select **RSI** from the built-in list.
- Modify the **Period**, **Line Colors**, and **Levels** (70/30 default).
- Apply it to different panels or overlay it with other tools like Bollinger Bands or volume indicators.
- NinjaTrader supports **RSI scripting** using NinjaScript for customized backtesting and automation.

Adjusting RSI to Fit Your Trading Strategy

- **Short-Term Scalping**:
    - Use RSI length of **5–9** for faster signals.
    - Consider overbought/oversold at **80/20** to avoid false reversals.
- **Swing Trading**:
    - Stick with classic **14-period** RSI.
    - Use 70/30 or 75/25 levels depending on volatility.

- **Trend Following**:
    - Add a **moving average to RSI** (e.g. 5-period MA of RSI).
    - Use crossovers or confluence with price structure.
- **Multi-Timeframe Trading**:
    - Plot RSI from a higher timeframe (e.g. 1-hour RSI on a 5-min chart).
    - Use this to filter trades—only take long trades when higher-timeframe RSI is above 50, for example.

Tips for Display Optimization

- Keep RSI **visually clean**—use contrasting colors and avoid overloading the panel.
- Add horizontal lines at **50**, **30**, and **70** for easy reference.
- Some traders prefer shaded backgrounds between 30 and 70 to emphasize "neutral zones."
- Use alerts to notify you when RSI hits key thresholds.

Summary

Setting up RSI correctly on your platform is the first step toward mastering it as a tool. Most platforms make it easy to add and customize RSI, but knowing how to tailor it to your strategy gives you a professional edge. Whether you're scalping on TradingView, building algo systems in MT5, or swing trading in Thinkorswim, a properly configured RSI setup helps you filter trades, identify reversals, and stay in sync with market momentum.

Key Takeaways

➢ RSI is available on all major platforms, including TradingView, MT4/5, Thinkorswim, and NinjaTrader.

➢ Customizing the RSI length and overbought/oversold thresholds allows you to align the indicator with your trading style.

➢ Different platforms offer powerful features such as scripting, multi-timeframe RSI, and conditional alerts.

➢ Display settings like line color, alert levels, and moving averages on RSI can improve clarity and usability.

➢ Always test RSI settings in a simulated or backtested environment before applying them live.

Chapter 4

Mastering RSI Entry and Exit Signals – How to Trade With Precision

Introduction

One of the most powerful uses of the Relative Strength Index (RSI) is for generating precise entry and exit signals. While many traders simply wait for RSI to cross the 70 or 30 thresholds, those who truly master the indicator understand the subtleties behind these moves—and how to stack the odds in their favor.

This chapter goes beyond the basics and dives deep into **RSI-based entry and exit strategies**, covering traditional signals, advanced setups, multi-timeframe filtering, and how to confirm signals with price action for maximum precision.

Understanding RSI Thresholds and What They Really Mean

- The classic RSI levels of **70 (overbought)** and **30 (oversold)** signal potential reversals, but they don't always mean "buy" or "sell" outright.

- In strong trends, RSI can stay overbought or oversold for extended periods—entering too early can lead to losses.

- Instead of viewing 70/30 as automatic reversal zones, think of them as **"extreme momentum warnings"** that need confirmation.

RSI Entry Signals – Beyond the Basics

RSI Crosses Below 30

- A potential **long signal**—suggests price is entering an oversold level and a potential upwards move.
- Best used in an uptrend or range-bound environment.
- Confirm with a strong bullish candlestick and/or volume spike.

Example:

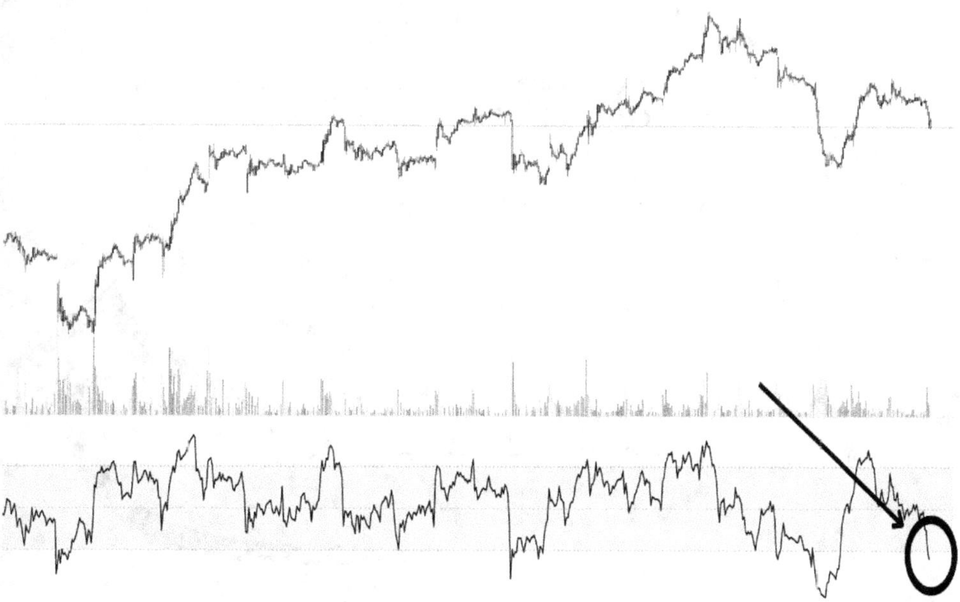

RSI crosses below 30 during an uptrend, signaling price is oversold

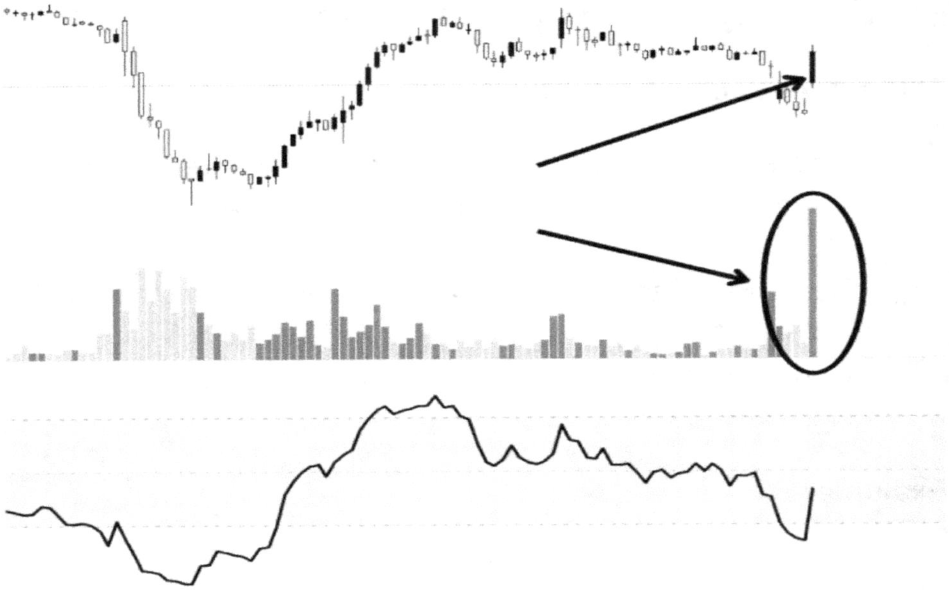

A strong bullish candlestick & a spike in volume confirm the move upwards, enter long at the close of the bullish candlestick

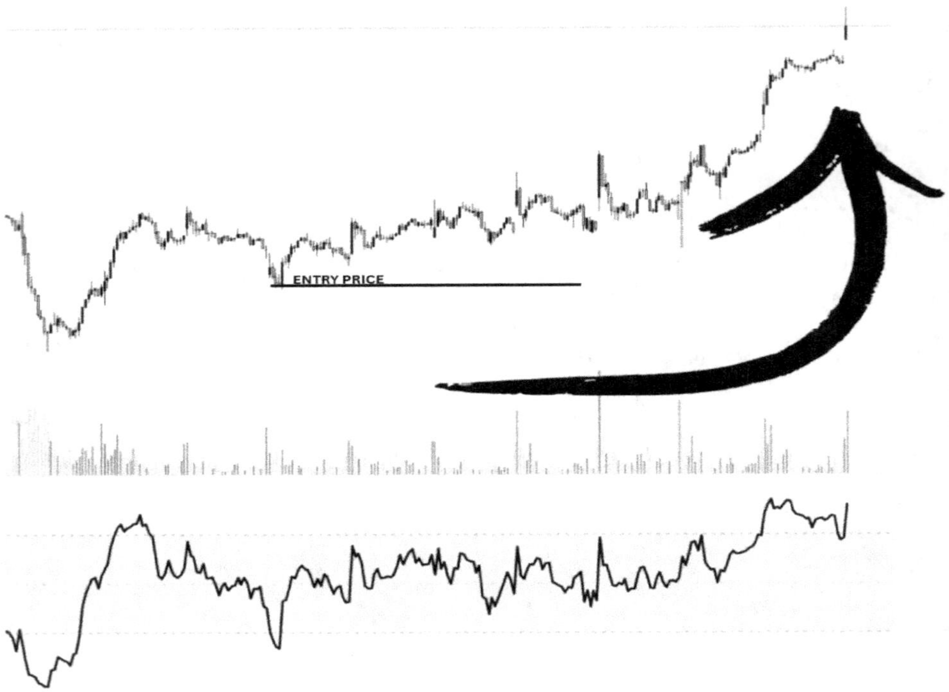

Chart shows a strong move to the upside

RSI Crosses Above 70

- A potential **short signal**—price is entering overbought territory and a potential downwards move.
- Works best in downtrends or sideways zones.
- Confirm with a strong bearish candlestick and/or volume spike.

Example:

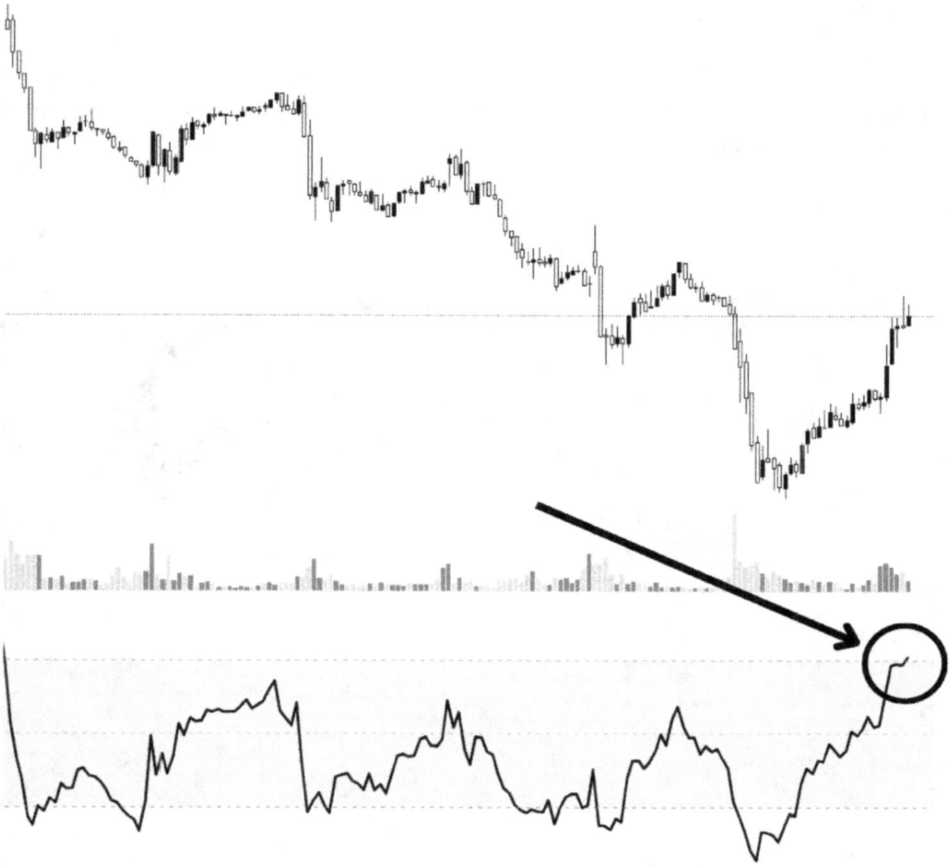

RSI crosses above 70 during a downtrend, signaling price is overbought

A strong bearish candlestick & spike in volume confirm the move downwards, enter short at the close of the bearish candlestick

Chart shows a strong move to the downside

RSI Midline Cross (50 Level)

- RSI crossing above 50 = rising momentum → possible long trigger, confirm with price showing an uptrend.

Example:

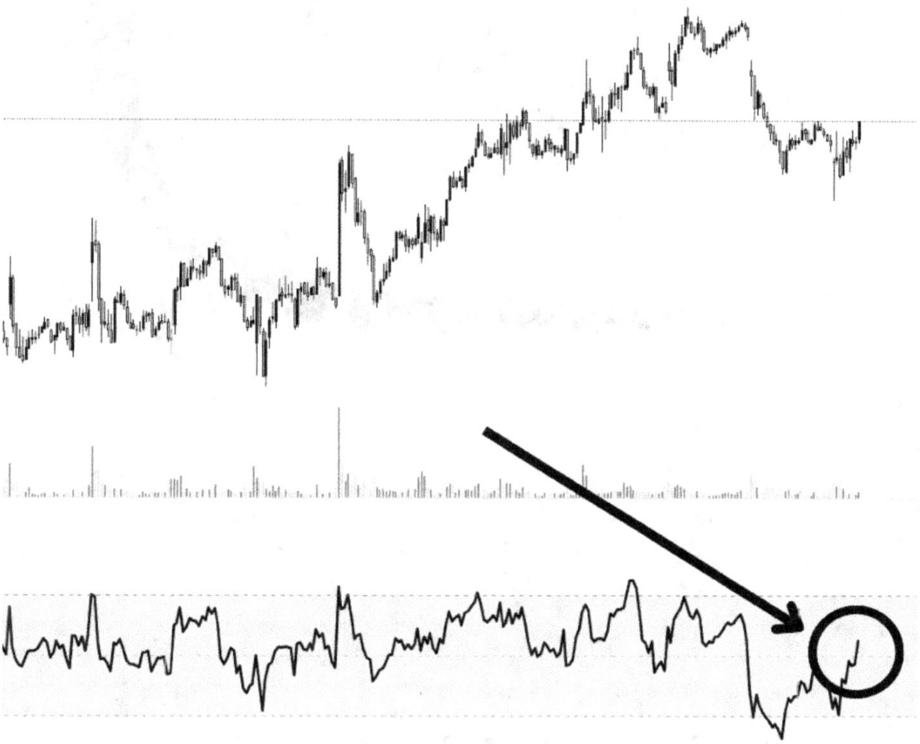

RSI crosses above 50 in an uptrend signaling rising momentum to the upside, enter long as soon RSI closes above 50

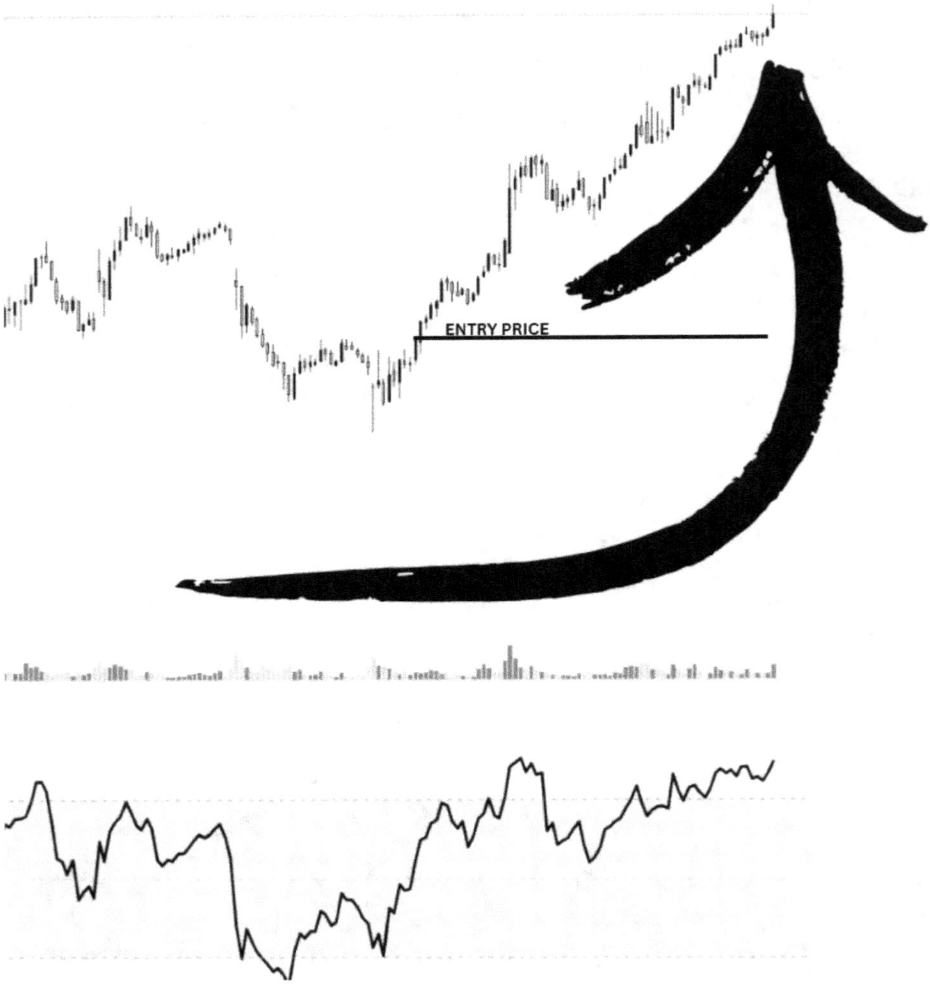

Chart shows a strong move to the upside, continuing the uptrend

- RSI crossing below 50 = weakening strength → possible short trigger, confirm with price showing a downtrend.

Example:

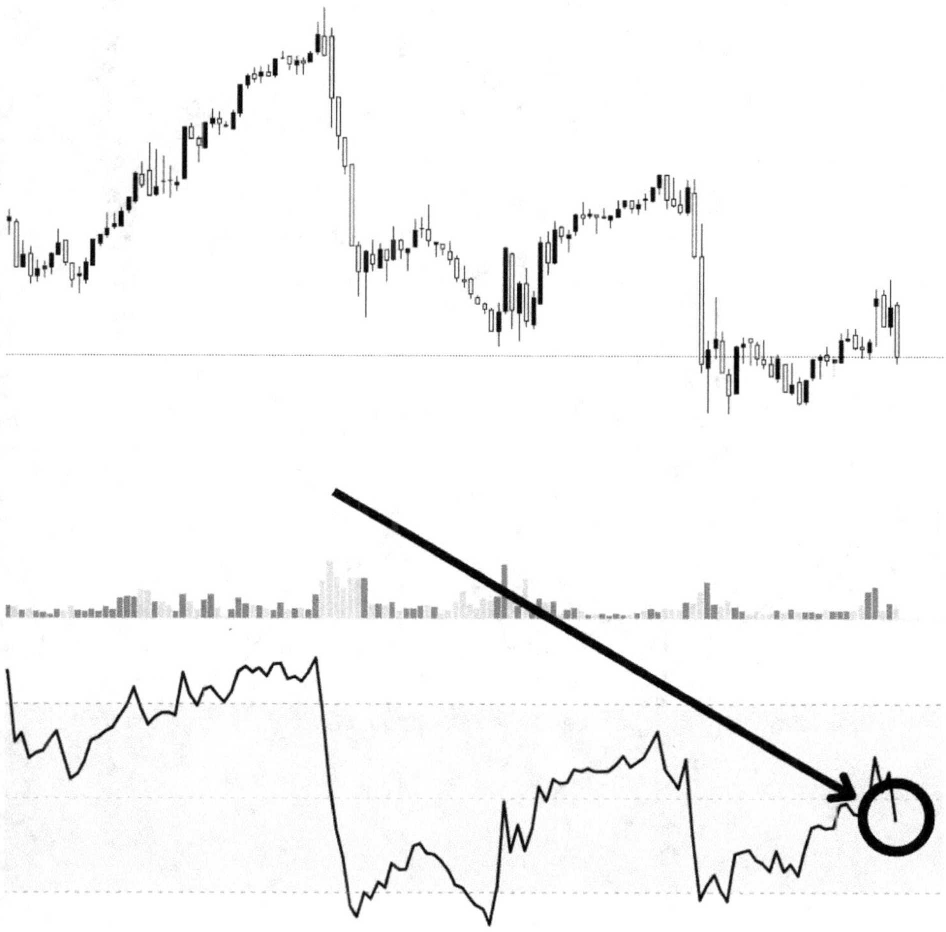

RSI crosses below 50 in a downtrend signaling rising momentum to the downside, enter short as soon as RSI closes below 50

Chart shows a strong move to the downside, continuing the downtrend

RSI Exit Strategies

Overbought/Oversold Exits

- Use 70/30 not just as entries, but **exits**—lock in profits when RSI enters extreme zones.
- Especially useful in range trading or swing positions.
- Avoid exiting just because RSI hits 70/30—wait for signs of momentum slowing (e.g. small candles, low volume).

Example (long):

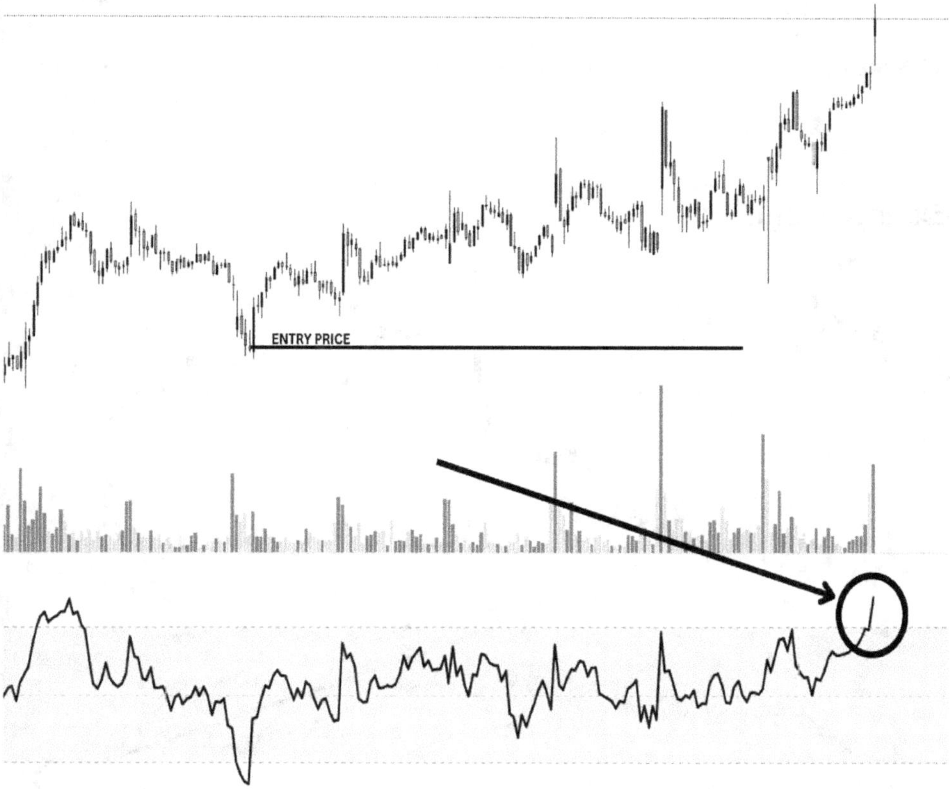

RSI crosses above 70 with a current long position, signaling price is overbought

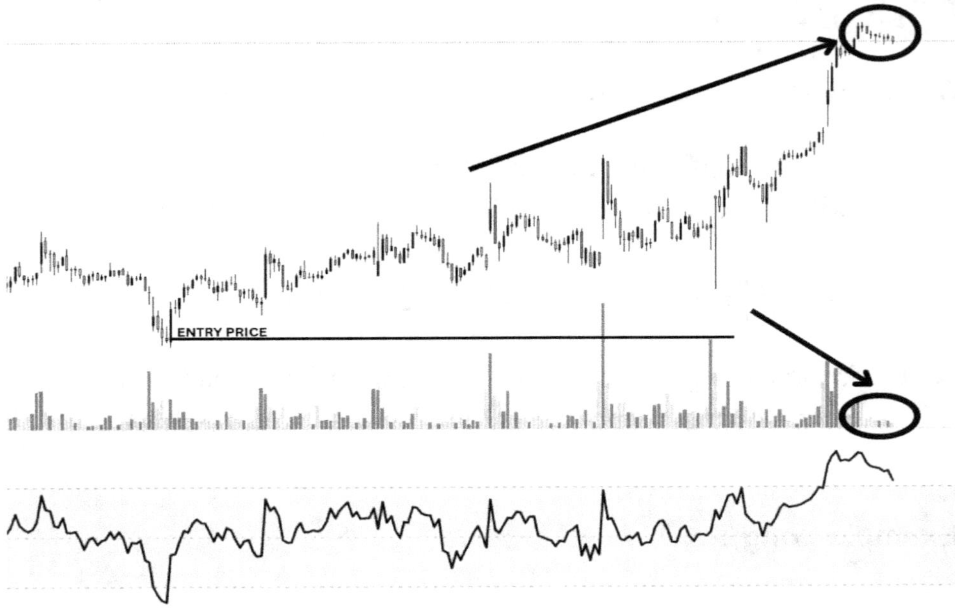

Small candles and low volume confirm price is overbought, exit long position here

Example (short):

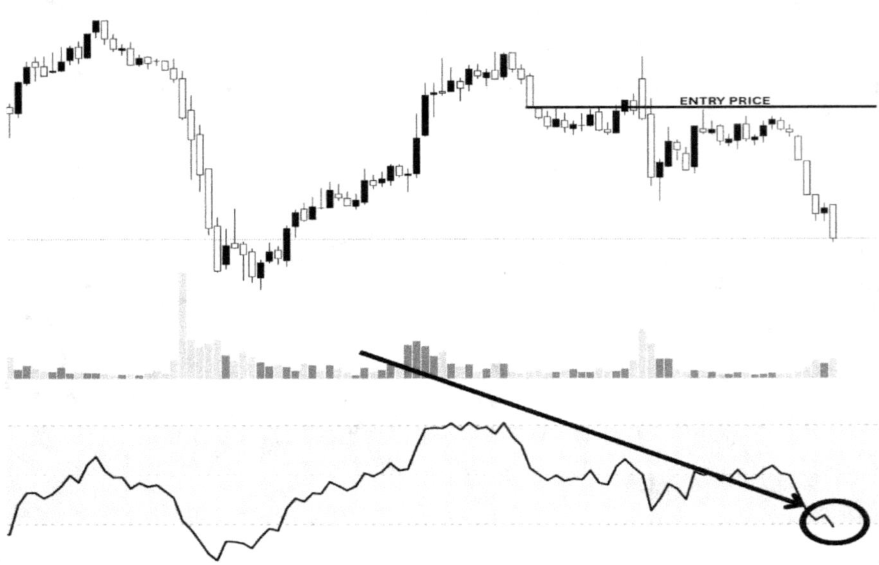

RSI crosses below 30 with a current short position, signaling price is oversold

Small candles and low volume confirm price is oversold, exit short position here

RSI Trailing Stop Technique

- Exit when RSI crosses back below a certain level (e.g. drop from above 70 to below 50 in a long trade, or rise from below 30 to above 50 in a short trade).
- This lets you **ride momentum** longer while protecting gains when strength fades.
- Use in combination with a **RSI midline cross entry** for best results.

Example (long):

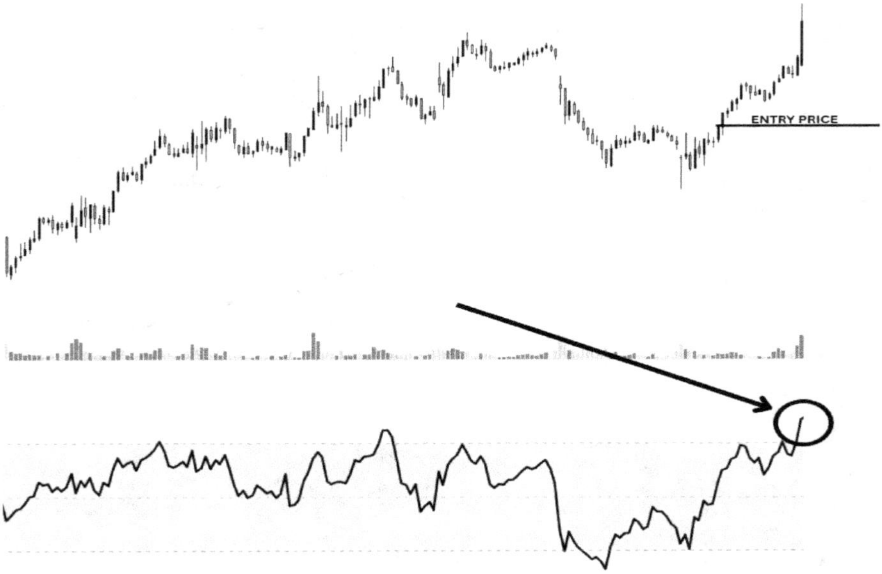

RSI crosses above 70 with a current long position, signaling momentum to the upside is fading

RSI falls back below 50 confirming momentum to the upside is fading, exit long position as soon as RSI closes below 50

Example (short):

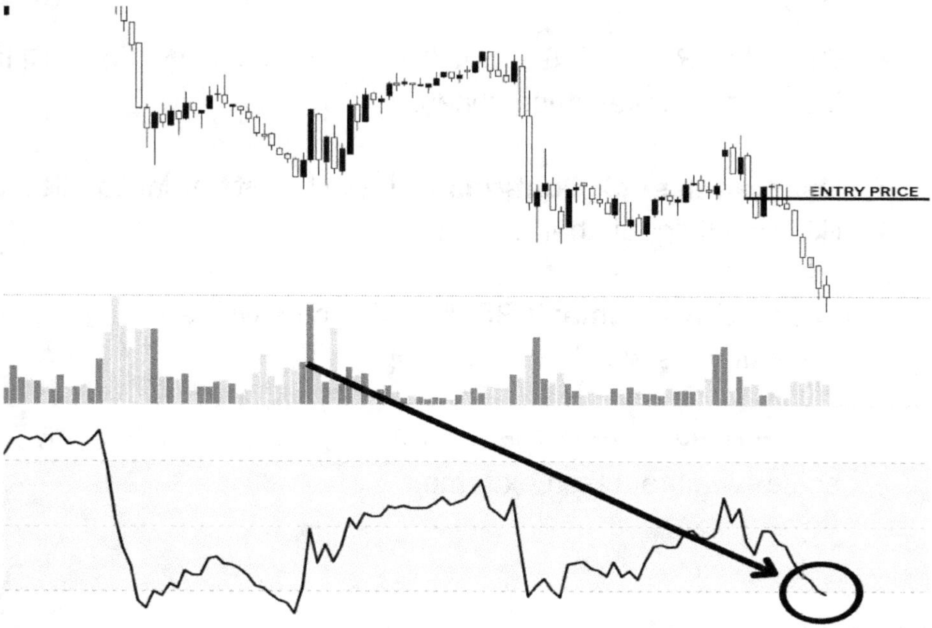

RSI crosses below 30 with a current short position, signaling momentum to the downside is fading

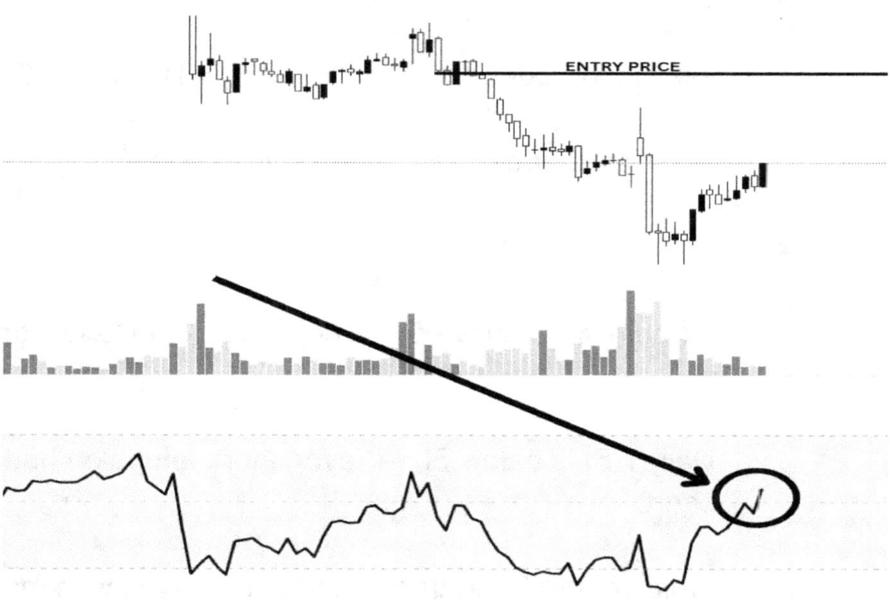

RSI rises back above 50 confirming momentum to the downside is fading, exit short position as soon as RSI closes above 50

RSI Signal Filtering – Avoiding False Triggers

- **Combine RSI with Support/Resistance**: Only act on RSI if it occurs near key price zones.
- **Use Candlestick Confirmation**: Wait for reversal candles like engulfing, pin bar, or doji.
- **Layer with Volume**: If RSI signal occurs with a volume spike, it adds weight to the setup.
- **Avoid Mid-Range Triggers**: RSI between 40–60 is often noise—wait for clean extremes.

RSI Multi-Timeframe Confirmation

- Use **higher timeframe RSI (HTF)** to filter trades:
    - Take long trades on LTF only when HTF RSI > 50.
    - Take short trades on LTF only when HTF RSI < 50.
- Example:
    - 1-hour RSI is above 50 → consider 5-min long signals only.
    - Daily RSI is below 50 → favor short setups on hourly chart.
- Helps avoid countertrend trades and stay in sync with macro flow.

RSI Entry and Exit Examples by Market

Oil Futures (CL)

- Use RSI 5 or 7 on 1-min or 5-min chart for **short-term scalps**.
- Look for RSI divergence at intraday highs/lows to fade blow-off moves.

Gold Futures (GC)

- Works well with **14-period RSI** and horizontal levels.
- Entry on RSI bounce off 30 near trendline support during pullback.

S&P 500 Futures (ES)

- Use RSI **with VWAP**—fade extremes when RSI diverges from price above/below VWAP.
- Combine RSI with market structure (e.g. lower high + RSI divergence = short trigger).

Nasdaq Futures (NQ)

- Use 2-minute RSI with 7-period setting during morning session.
- Confirm RSI breakout setups with bullish engulfing near 50-cross.

Summary

Mastering RSI entries and exits is about more than just watching numbers cross a line—it's about learning to interpret momentum in context. By combining RSI signals with price action, volume, market structure, and multi-timeframe alignment, you can transform a simple indicator into a precise trading tool. Whether you're fading exhaustion in gold or timing a breakout in oil, strategic RSI use allows you to enter with confidence and exit with discipline.

Key Takeaways

➤ RSI thresholds (70/30) are guidelines—not guaranteed reversal signals. Always confirm with price action.

➤ Entry signals include RSI crosses, divergence, and 50-line trend confirmations.

➤ Exit strategies using RSI include overbought/oversold profit-taking, RSI crossbacks, and divergence signs.

➤ RSI works best when combined with candlestick patterns, support/resistance, and volume.

➤ Multi-timeframe RSI filtering helps you stay in sync with larger trends and avoid whipsaws.

Chapter 5

RSI and Trend Analysis – Using RSI to Confirm Trend Strength and Direction

Introduction

While the Relative Strength Index (RSI) is often seen as a reversal tool, it can also be a powerful way to confirm and ride trends. In trending markets—especially in futures like oil, gold, and indexes—RSI helps you identify momentum strength, avoid premature exits, and confirm that a trend is still alive.

This chapter will show you how to use RSI as a **trend-following filter**, a momentum gauge, and a confidence booster to stay in profitable trades longer—and avoid getting chopped up in weak setups.

Using RSI as a Trend Filter

- RSI can act as a **"trend filter"** to help determine if you should be looking for buys or sells.
- When RSI stays above **50**, it confirms bullish momentum and favors **long setups**.

Example:

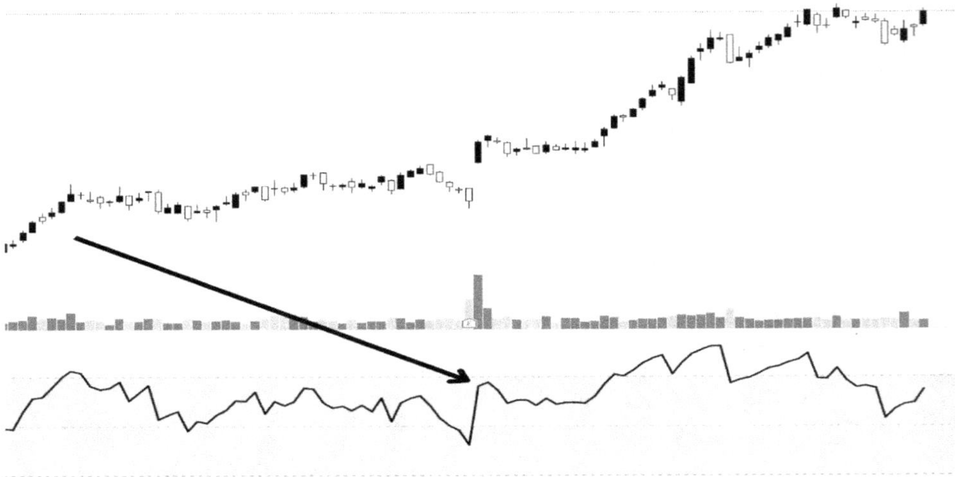

RSI staying above 50 confirms an uptrend and bullish momentum

- When RSI stays below **50**, it confirms bearish pressure and favors **short setups**.

Example:

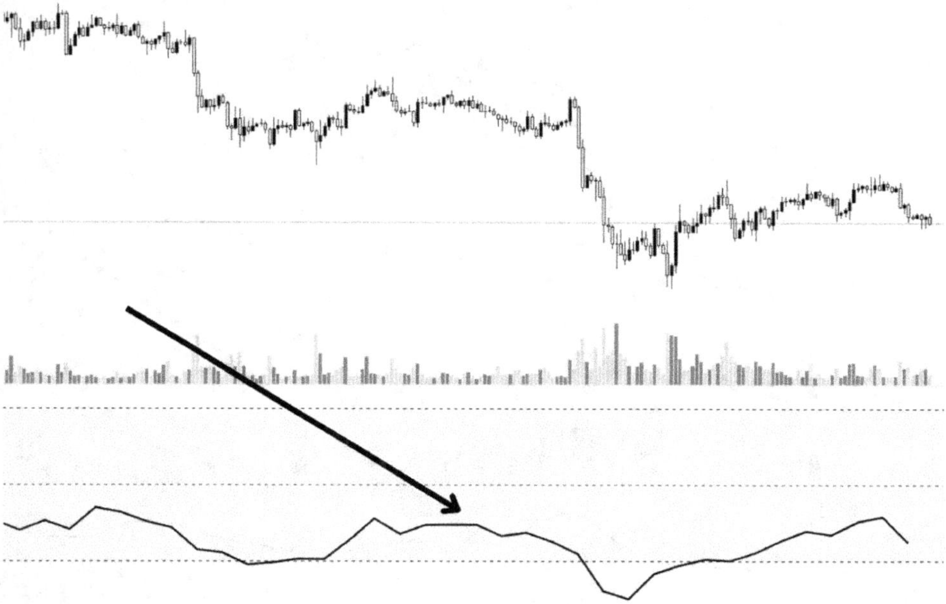

RSI staying below 50 confirms a downtrend and bearish momentum

- In very strong trends, RSI may stay above **70** or below **30** for extended periods.

Example (uptrend):

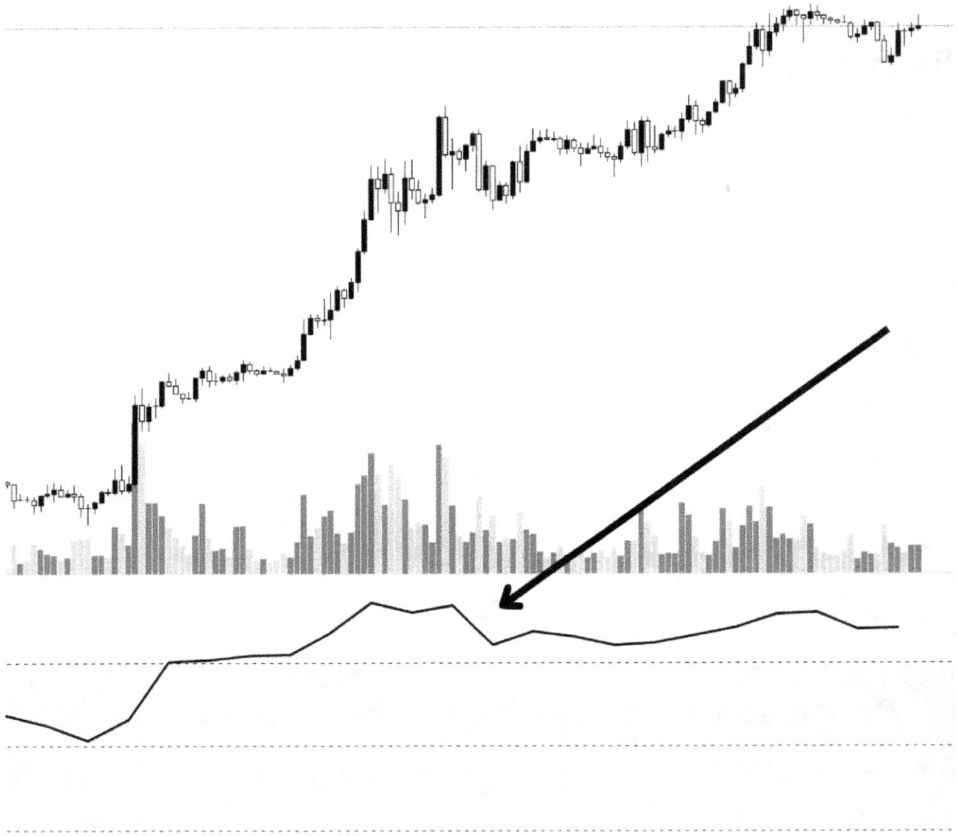

RSI staying above 70 for an extended period of time confirms a strong uptrend and bullish momentum

Example (downtrend):

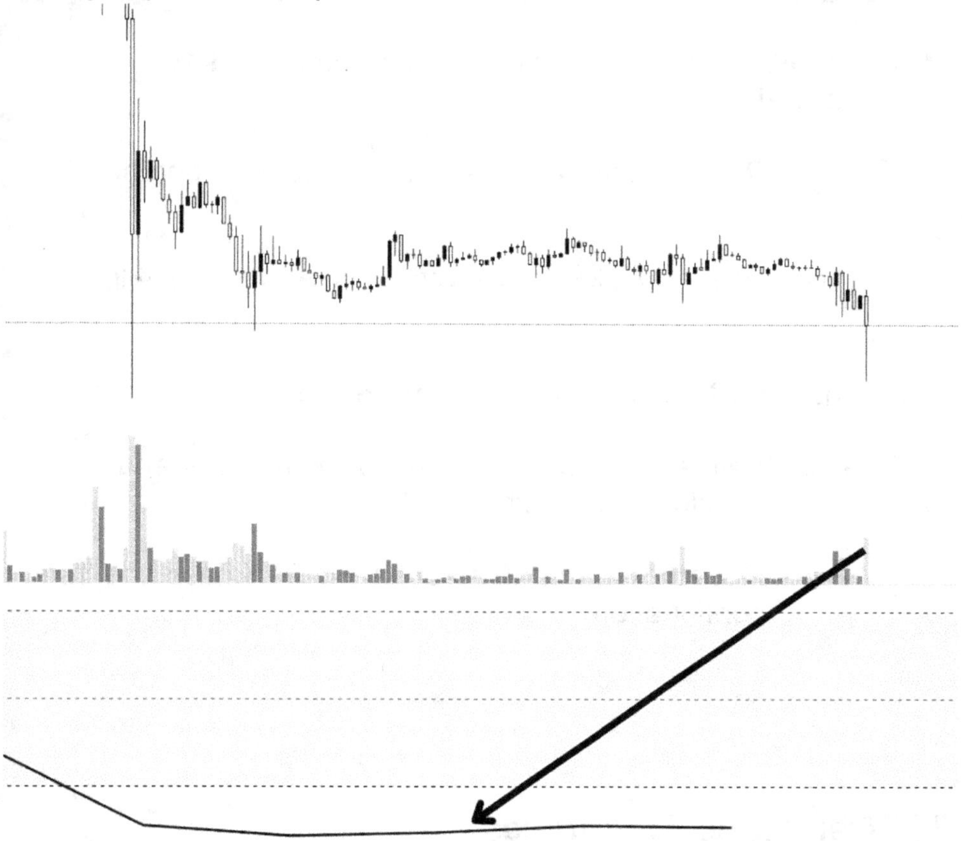

RSI staying below 30 for an extended period of time confirms a strong downtrend and bearish momentum

- Avoid countertrend trades when RSI confirms that the dominant momentum is still strong.

RSI and Trend Strength Zones

- The **40–90 range** often indicates **bullish market conditions**:
  - RSI dips into 40–50 = trend pullback → potential long entry.
  - RSI stays between 60–70 = strong uptrend with continuation.
- The **10–60 range** indicates **bearish pressure**:
  - RSI rallies into 50–60 = pullback in downtrend → possible short entry.
  - RSI stuck under 40 = confirmed weakness and trend continuation.

RSI Trend Line Techniques

- Draw **trendlines** on the RSI indicator itself—breakouts from these trendlines can signal changes in momentum.
- RSI trendline break + price breaking structure = **powerful reversal or acceleration signal**.
- RSI trendlines often break **before** price trendlines, giving early momentum clues.

Example:

RSI and price both respecting an uptrend line

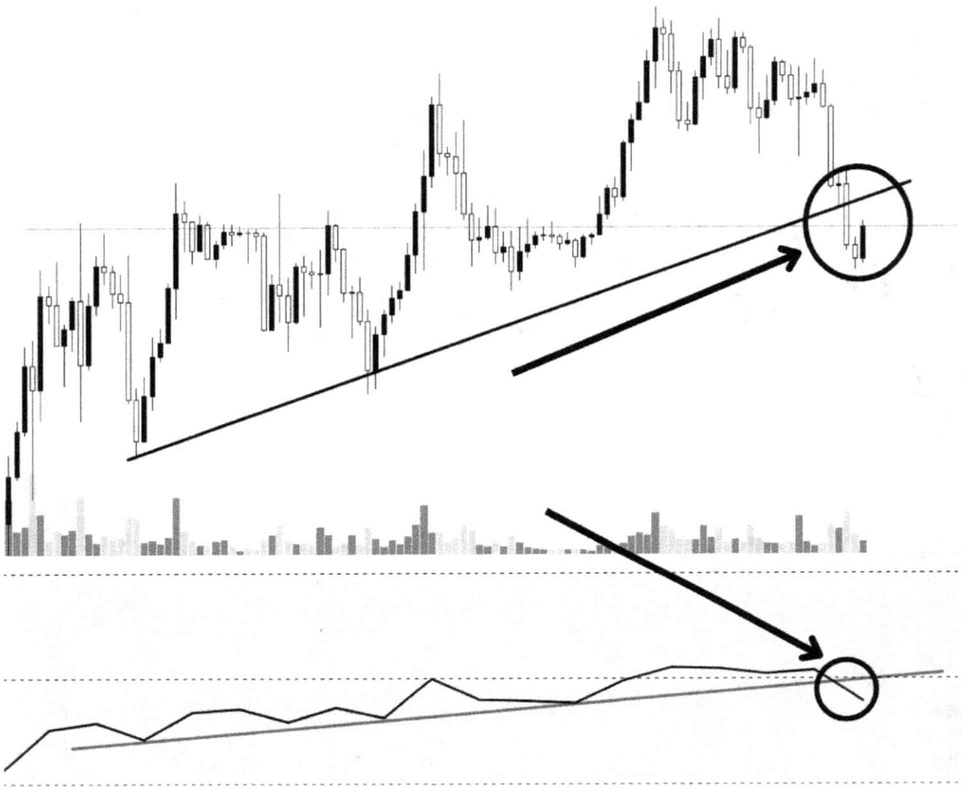

RSI and price both break below the uptrend lines, signaling a reversal to the downside

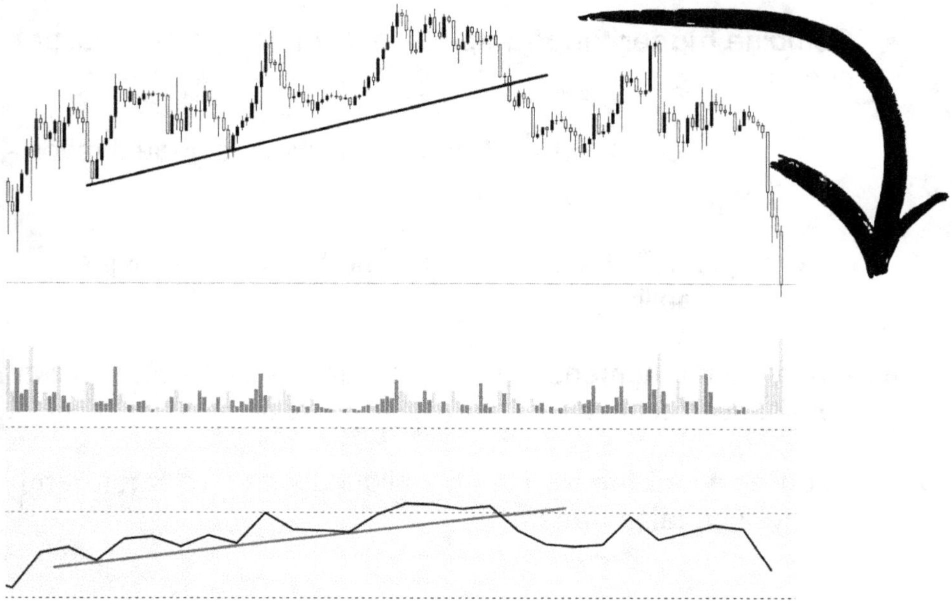

Chart shows a strong move to the downside

RSI Trend Confirmation in Different Timeframes

- Combine **higher timeframe RSI** to filter setups on smaller charts:
    - Daily RSI > 60 = intraday trend signals should favor longs.
    - 4-hour RSI < 50 = 15-min short setups are higher probability.
- Avoid fading momentum when higher timeframe RSI shows dominant direction.
- Use **RSI as a bias tool** to stay aligned with the larger trend and reduce false trades.

Market Examples

Oil Futures (CL)

- In strong oil uptrends, RSI holds between **60–75** for hours or days.
- Look for pullbacks to 50–60 zone on RSI for continuation trades.
- Avoid fading moves unless RSI breaks below 50 and price confirms with structure break.

Gold Futures (GC)

- RSI 14 often ranges from **40–60** in sideways conditions—avoid trend trades in this zone.

- A clean break and hold above 60 on RSI suggests bullish trend development.
- Use RSI to ride trends by trailing stops as long as RSI remains above 55.

S&P 500 Futures (ES)

- RSI trend bias (e.g., daily RSI > 60) filters your intraday trades.
- In rallies, RSI frequently bounces at 50–60—re-enter on pullbacks near these zones.
- Avoid short trades while RSI is embedded above 65.

Nasdaq Futures (NQ)

- High momentum = RSI readings of **70+** are normal and sustainable.
- Don't short just because RSI is "overbought"—wait for a breakdown below 50.
- Use RSI slope as a **momentum strength gauge**—steep upward slope confirms trend strength.

Summary

When used as a trend tool, RSI becomes a valuable asset for confirming bias, avoiding bad countertrend trades, and giving you the confidence to stay in winning positions. Instead of only using RSI for reversal signals, the savvy trader uses it to align with trend direction, identify pullback zones, and anticipate momentum shifts. By anchoring your strategy to the behavior of RSI during trends, you enhance your precision and consistency across all futures markets.

Key Takeaways

➢ RSI above 50 suggests bullish momentum; below 50 suggests bearish pressure.

➢ In trends, RSI often remains elevated or suppressed—this confirms strength, not reversal.

➢ Use RSI zones like 40–60 for entries and midline crosses (50) to manage bias.

➢ Drawing trendlines on RSI can reveal early signs of a trend shift.

➢ Pair RSI trend analysis with higher timeframe bias and market structure for maximum accuracy.

Chapter 6

RSI Divergence Mastery – Spotting Reversals Before They Happen

Introduction

One of the most powerful uses of the Relative Strength Index (RSI) is spotting divergences—subtle clues that momentum is fading and a potential price reversal is near. While price might be making new highs or lows, RSI can warn you that the move is weakening. This chapter will show you how to identify bullish and bearish divergence across all major futures markets and use it to catch high-probability turning points before the crowd.

What Is RSI Divergence?

- Divergence occurs when **price action and RSI move in opposite directions**.
- It signals a **disconnect between price and momentum**, often preceding a reversal.
- There are two primary types:
    - **Bullish Divergence**: Price makes a lower low, but RSI makes a higher low, signals that momentum downwards is fading and a potential reversal to the upside.
    - **Bearish Divergence**: Price makes a higher high, but RSI makes a lower high, signals that momentum upwards is fading and a potential reversal to the downside.
- Divergence is especially powerful near **key support/resistance** or after extended trends.

How to Spot Bullish Divergence

- Look for **downtrending markets** where price prints a **new low**, but RSI fails to confirm.
- A **higher low on RSI** suggests the selling pressure is weakening even as price drops.
- This is often the first sign of **smart money buying quietly into weakness**.

Example:

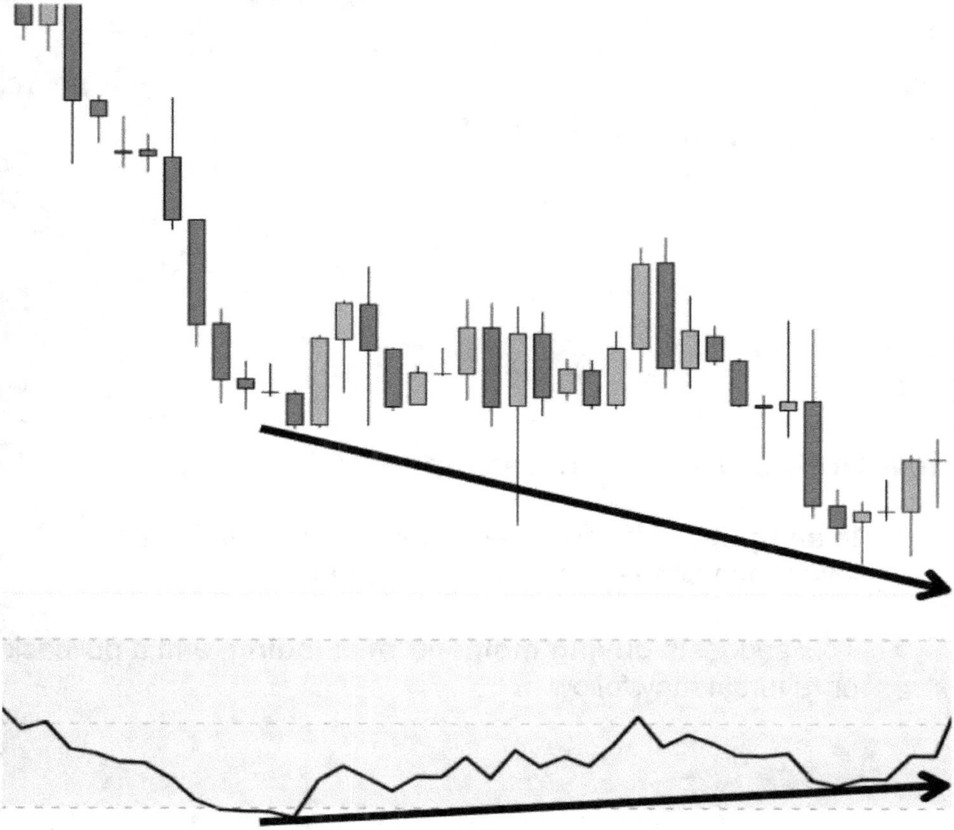

Price is in a downtrend and making lower lows while RSI is making higher lows, signaling a reversal to the upside

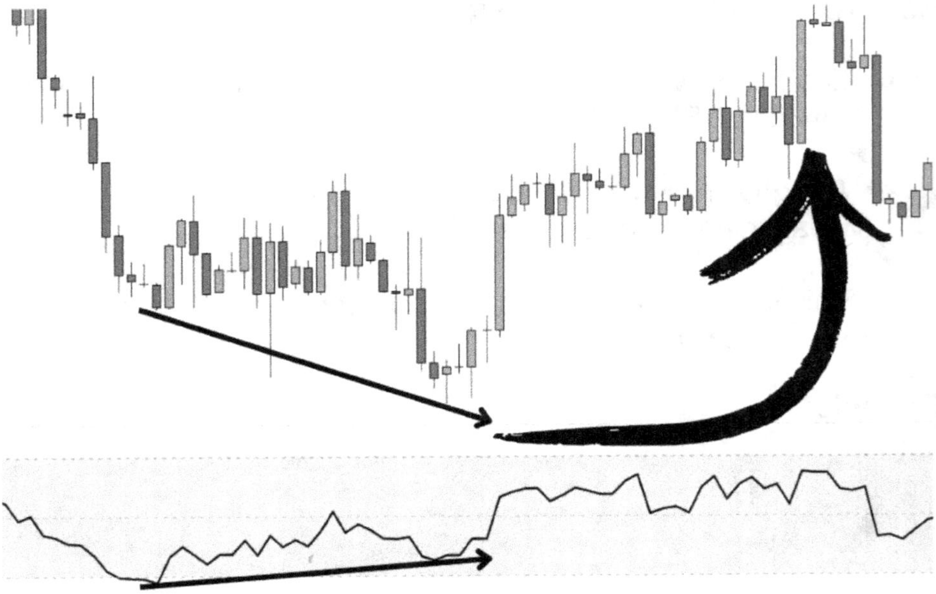

Chart shows a strong move to the upside

How to Spot Bearish Divergence

- In an **uptrend**, if price makes a **new high** but RSI peaks lower than before, it's bearish divergence.
- This suggests **buying momentum is fading**, and a pullback or reversal may follow.

Example:

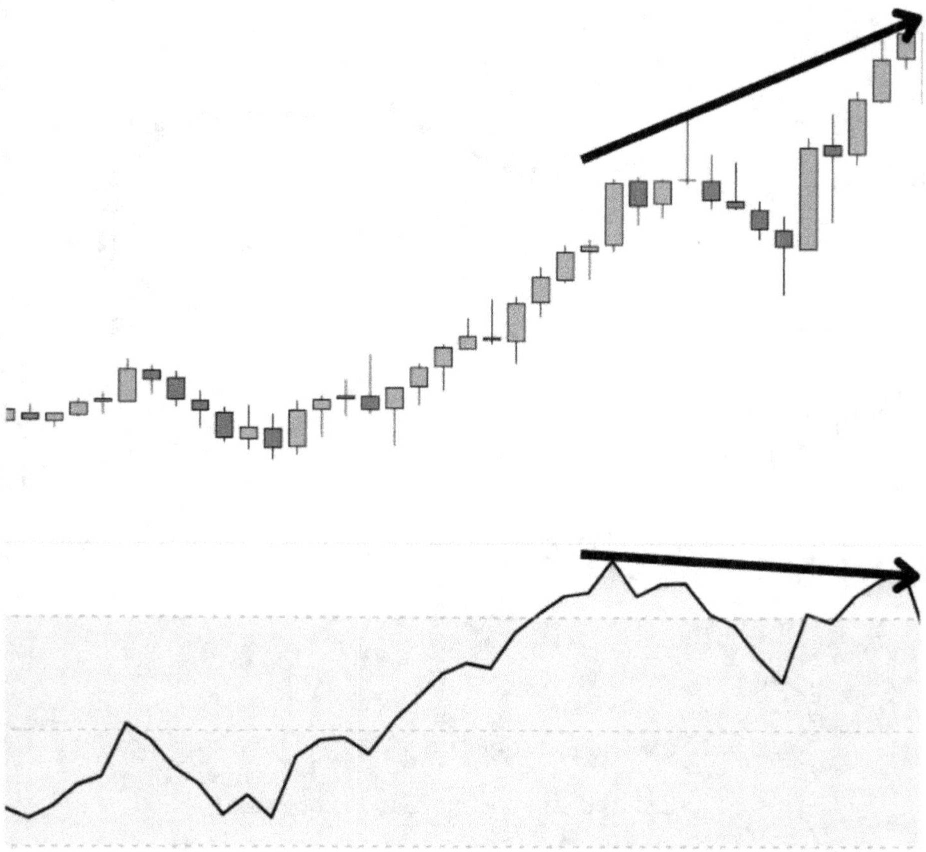

Price is in an uptrend and making higher highs while RSI is making lower highs, signaling a reversal to the downside

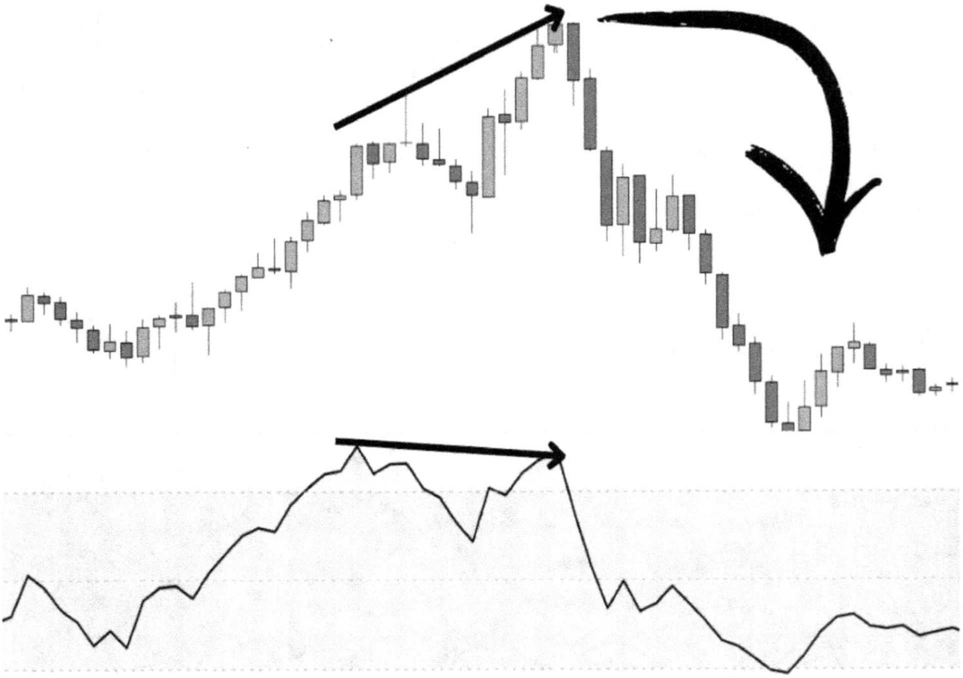

Chart shows a strong move to the downside

Confirming Divergence with Price Action

- Don't trade divergence **in isolation**—wait for **confirmation**:
  - A trendline break on price or RSI,
  - A candlestick pattern that shows momentum is shifting,
  - A break of a recent high or low that confirms a trend change.
- For futures, combine divergence with **volume profile**, **VWAP**, or **support zones** for higher conviction.

RSI Divergence in Different Timeframes

- Divergence is more powerful on **higher timeframes** like the 4-hour or daily.
- On lower timeframes (1-min, 5-min), use it for **quick scalps or confirmation**.
- For swing trading, weekly RSI divergence can mark **major turning points** in futures markets.

Summary

Divergence is one of the most effective tools to anticipate reversals **before they become obvious**. Whether you're catching tops, bottoms, or pullbacks, spotting when RSI disagrees with price gives you an edge few traders exploit properly. Combine divergence with structure, volume, and market context for higher-quality trades. It can help you avoid late entries, improve timing, and stack the odds in your favor across oil, gold, and index futures.

Key Takeaways

➤ **RSI divergence** signals a mismatch between price and momentum—an early warning of a potential reversal.

➤ **Bullish divergence** occurs when price makes a lower low but RSI makes a higher low.

➤ **Bearish divergence** happens when price makes a higher high but RSI makes a lower high.

➤ Use divergence with price structure, candlestick patterns, and key zones for confirmation.

➤ **Hidden divergence** supports trend continuation and is ideal for pullback entries.

➤ Higher timeframe divergence carries more weight and can mark major turning points in futures markets.

Chapter 7

RSI in Consolidation – Trading the Range with Confidence

Introduction

Markets don't always trend. In fact, a large percentage of the time, they **consolidate in sideways ranges**—often frustrating traders who only look for breakouts or trending opportunities. The RSI shines in these conditions by identifying overbought and oversold levels **within a well-defined range**. In this chapter, you'll learn how to trade with confidence in choppy, range-bound markets using RSI as your guide.

Why RSI Is Ideal for Sideways Markets

- When markets are range-bound, **momentum oscillates**, making RSI's signals especially reliable.
- RSI gives you **mean reversion clues**, helping you buy low and sell high within the range.
- Unlike trend indicators that become noisy in chop, RSI remains **clear and structured** in sideways conditions.

How to Identify a Range-Bound Market

- Price moves **between two horizontal levels** without breaking out significantly.
- RSI oscillates consistently **between 30 and 70** or **40 and 60** depending on volatility.

- Common signs include:
    - Price rejection at support/resistance levels
    - Lack of higher highs or lower lows

Example:

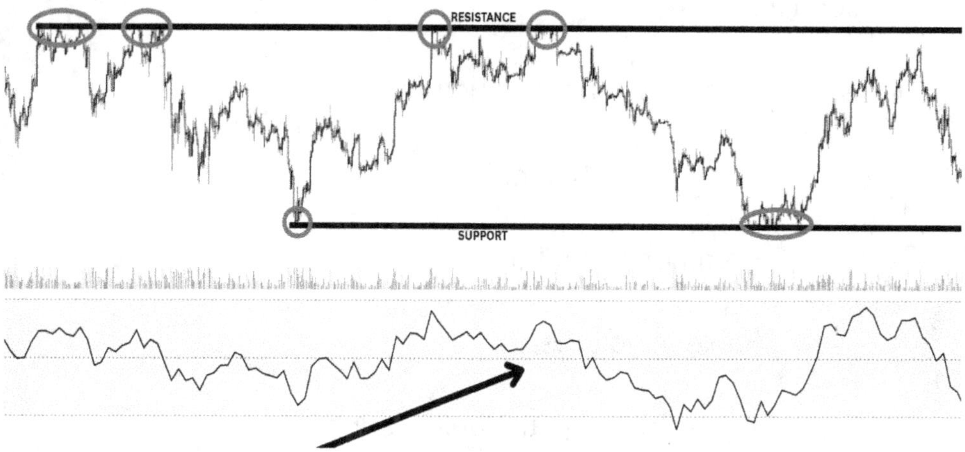

Price is rejecting support and resistance levels and not making higher highs or higher lows while RSI is consistently oscillating between 30 and 70, making it a range bound market

Setting RSI Parameters for Ranges

- The default RSI period of **14** works well, but you may tighten it to **8 or 10** for quicker entries.
- In lower-volatility ranges, use RSI levels of **40 and 60** as overbought/oversold zones.
- In wider, more volatile ranges, use the classic **30 and 70** thresholds.

Entry Strategies Using RSI in Ranges

Buying the Bottom of the Range

- Wait for price to approach a known **support zone**.
- Look for RSI to dip below **30**, signaling an oversold condition.
- Confirm with price action such as:
    - Strong bullish candle
    - Hammer or pin bar
    - Spike in volume
- Enter long with a stop just below support.

Example:

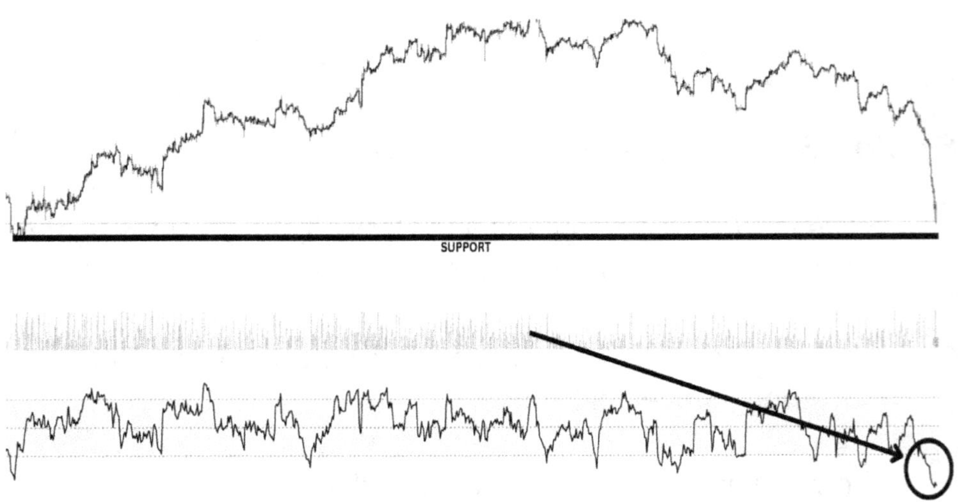

Price approaches support level and RSI dips below 30, signaling an oversold condition

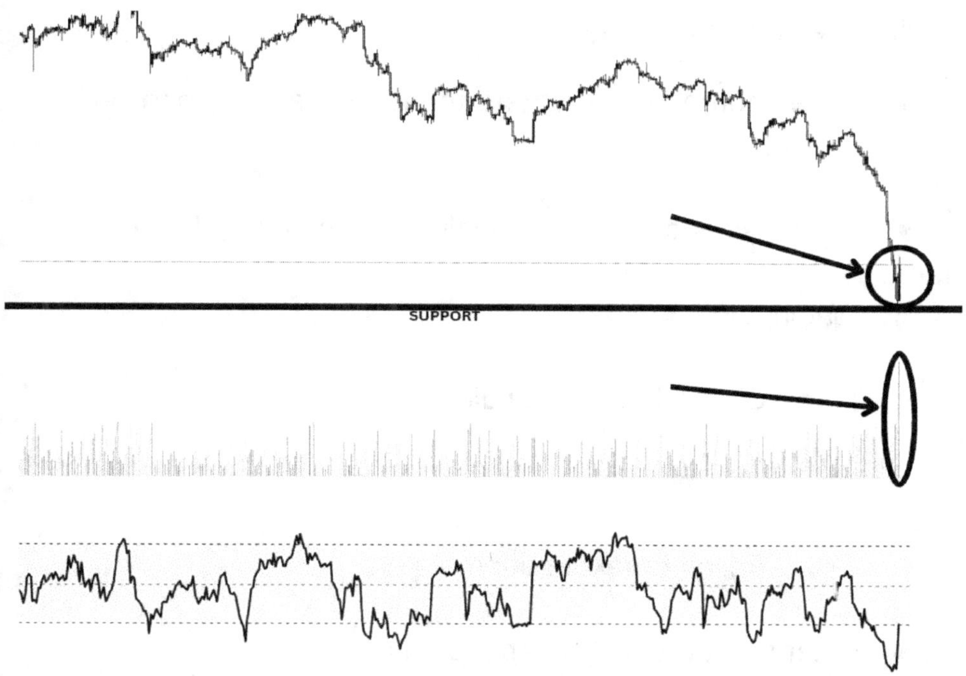

A strong bullish candlestick and a spike in volume confirm price is oversold and a potential move to the upside, enter long at the close of the strong bullish candlestick with a stop just below the support level

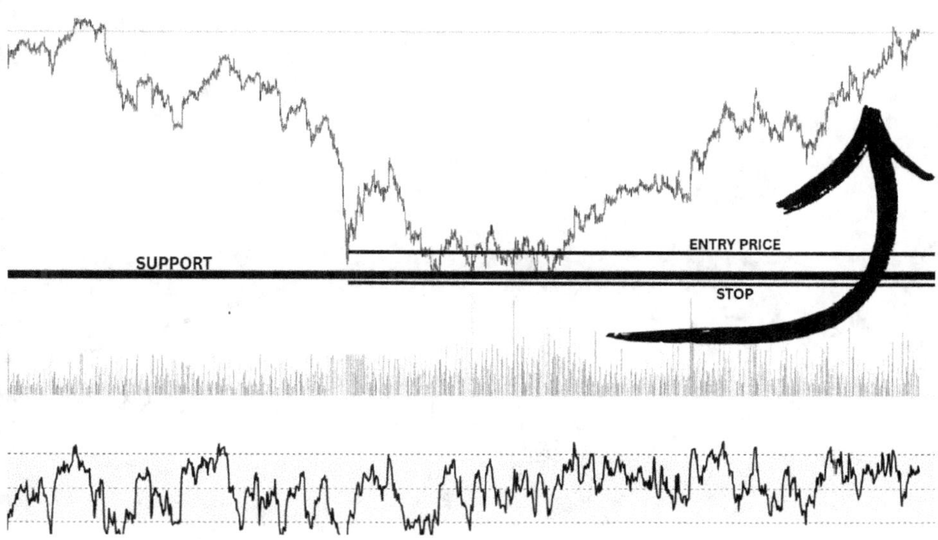

Chart shows a strong move to the upside

Selling the Top of the Range

- Price approaches a **resistance level** that's been tested before.
- RSI crosses above **70**, signaling an overbought condition.
- Watch for:
    - Strong bearish candles
    - Volume spikes
    - Failed breakout attempts
- Enter short with a stop above resistance.

Example:

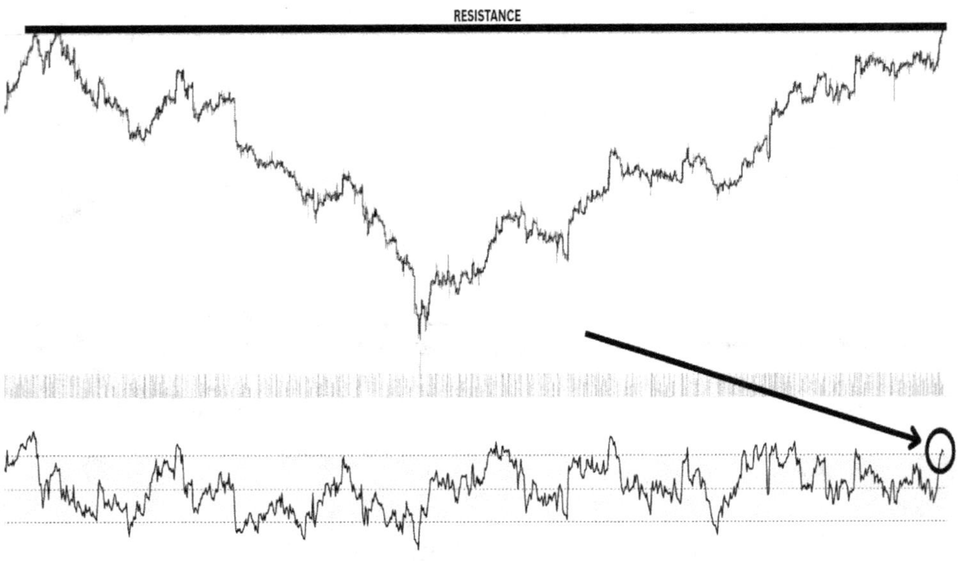

Price approaches resistance level and RSI dips above 70, signaling an overbought condition

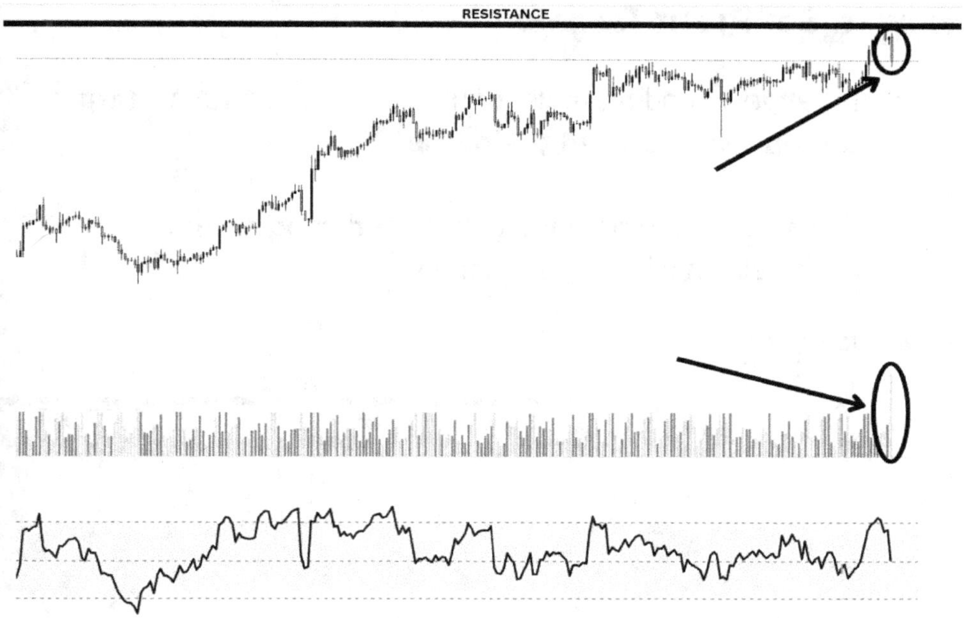

A strong bearish candlestick and a spike in volume confirm price is overbought and a potential move to the downside, enter short at the close of the strong bearish candlestick with a stop just above the resistance level

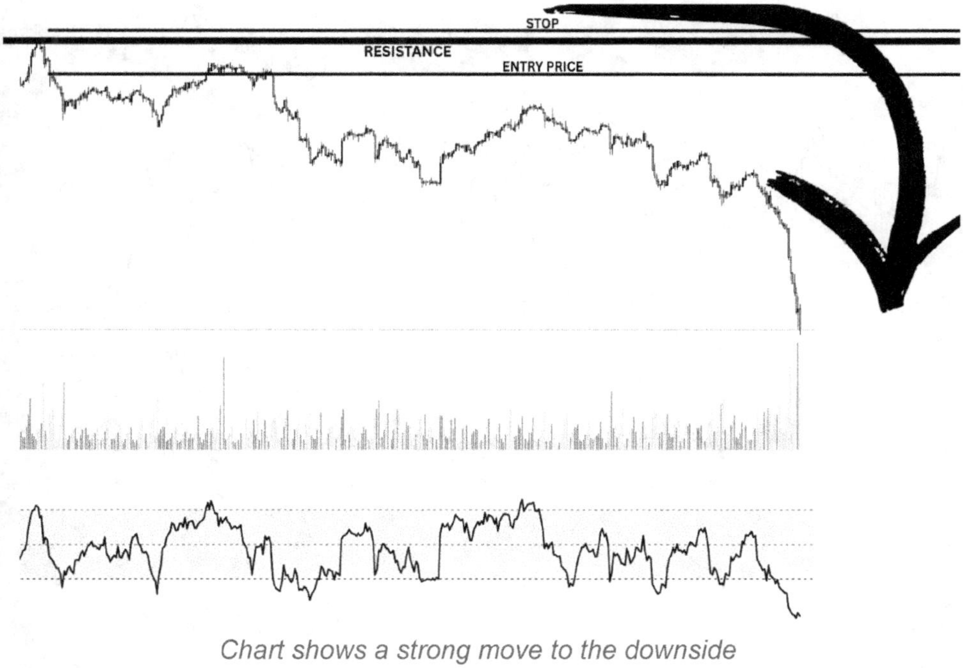

Chart shows a strong move to the downside

How to Set Profit Targets

- In range-bound markets, don't aim for home runs—**target the opposite side of the range**.
- Consider taking partial profits at **mid-range zones**, especially in wide consolidations.

Example (long):

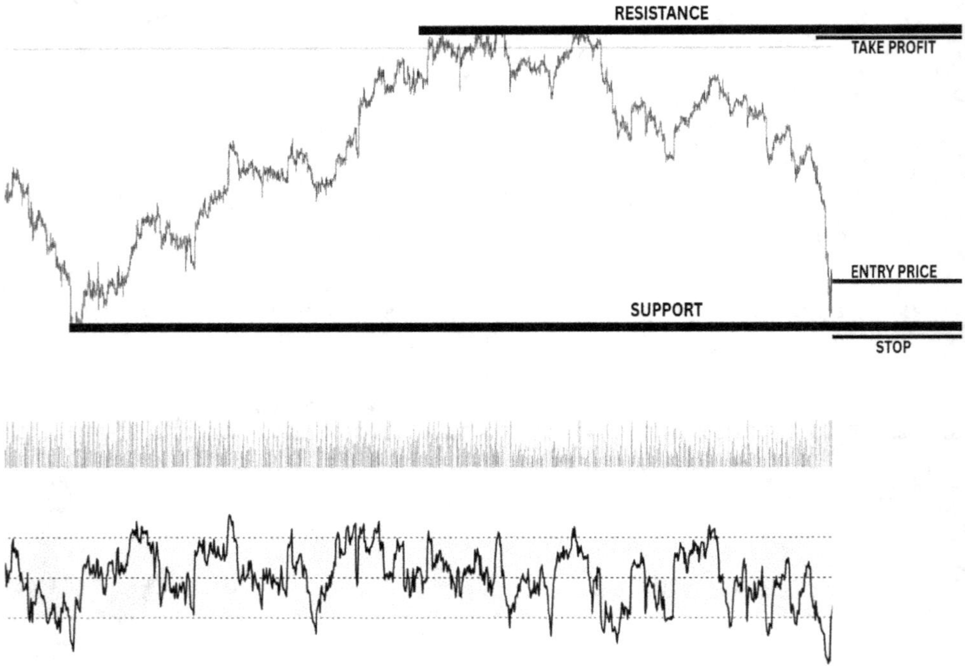

When entering long at a support level, set take profit to just under the resistance level

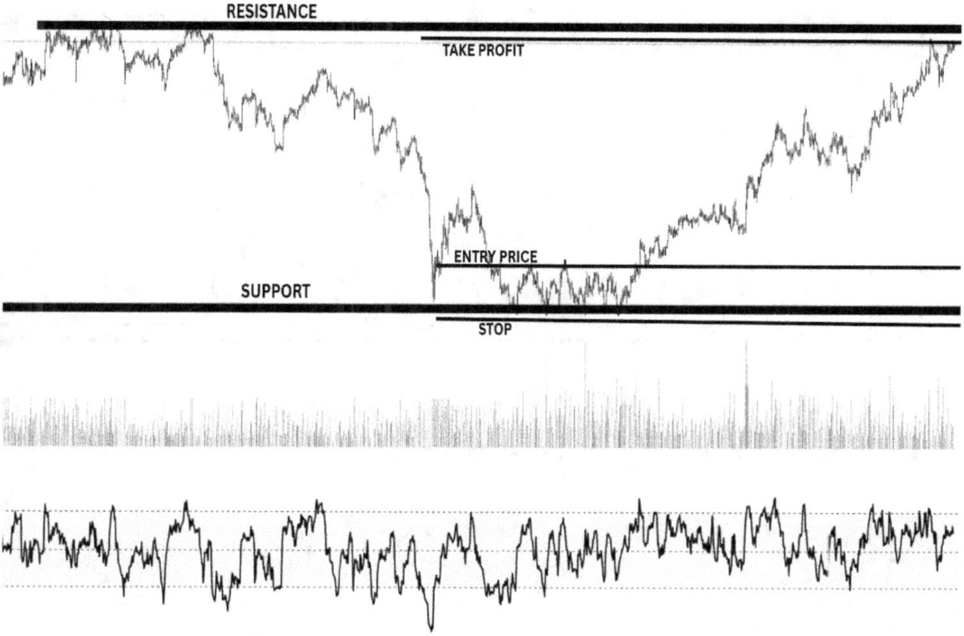

Chart shows a strong move to the upside towards resistance and hits take profit

Example (short):

When entering short at a resistance level, set take profit to just above the support level

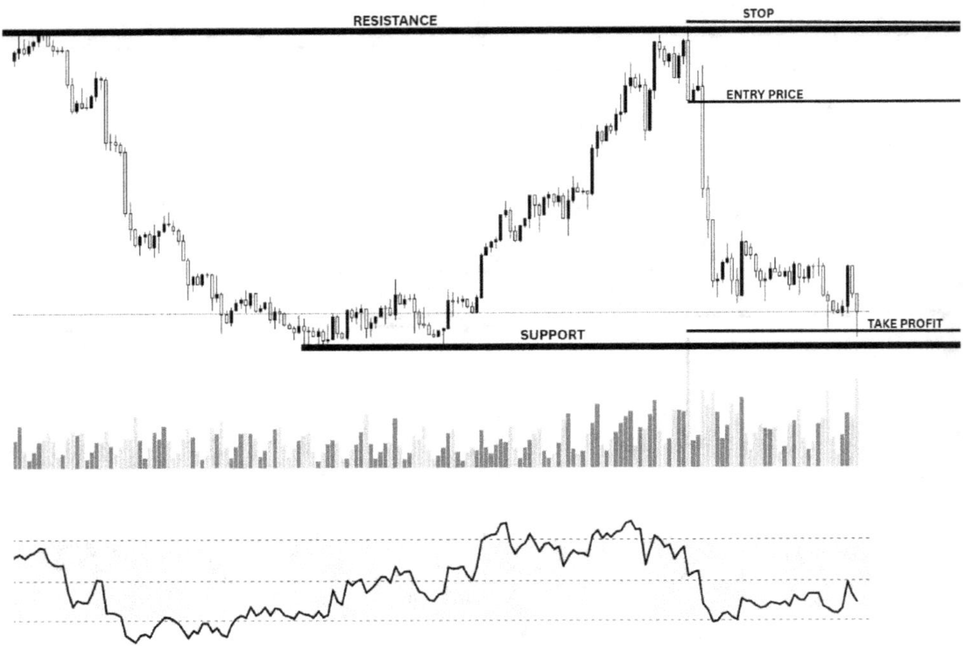

Chart shows a strong move to the downside towards support and hits take profit

Avoiding RSI Traps in Ranges

- Avoid entering too early—wait for **confirmation candles** and **clear RSI signals**.
- Be cautious when RSI hovers near 50; this often means the market is **indecisive**.
- If the range is too tight or erratic, **stand aside** and wait for clean structure.
- Avoid overtrading—limit to 1–2 quality trades per range cycle.

When to Stop Trading the Range

- Watch for:
    - RSI begins **breaking out of the 30–70 band** strongly,
    - Price closes outside the range with volume,
    - Moving averages begin sloping again,
- These signs mean a **trend may be emerging**. Time to switch strategy.

Summary

Trading in a consolidation phase doesn't have to be frustrating—**if you use RSI effectively**. This powerful oscillator thrives in sideways markets, offering clear overbought and oversold signals that let you confidently buy low and sell high. By combining RSI with clean support and resistance levels, candlestick confirmation, and risk-managed exits, you can profit steadily from otherwise "boring" market conditions. Mastering this will round out your skillset and keep you profitable in all market environments.

Key Takeaways

➤ RSI is most effective in **range-bound markets**, where it provides reliable mean reversion signals.

➤ Use RSI levels of **30/70 or 40/60** depending on range volatility and timeframe.

➤ Combine RSI with **support/resistance levels and candlestick confirmation** for entries.

➤ Exit trades at the **opposite end of the range**, using RSI re-crosses as signals.

➤ Avoid trades when RSI sits near 50 and price is directionless—wait for edge.

➤ Watch for breakout signs (RSI + price + volume) to shift away from range trading strategy.

Chapter 8

RSI Breakout Confirmation – Separating Fakeouts from Real Moves

Introduction

One of the biggest frustrations traders face is **false breakouts**—when price appears to break through support or resistance, only to reverse and trap traders. The RSI indicator can be a powerful ally in avoiding these traps by helping confirm **which breakouts are real** and which are likely to fail. In this chapter, you'll learn how to combine RSI with price action and volume to verify breakout strength across all major markets.

Why Breakouts Fail (and How RSI Helps)

- Many breakouts are **liquidity hunts** engineered to trigger stops and reverse.
- RSI helps confirm whether momentum is backing the move or if it's likely a **fakeout**.
- RSI provides early warning signs of a **loss of strength** or a **real momentum surge**.

Classic Signs of a False Breakout

- RSI does **not break out** with price (i.e., divergence).
- Price pierces resistance/support but **closes back inside** the range.
- Volume is **weak** during the breakout.
- Candlesticks show **reversal wicks** or engulfing patterns after the breakout attempt.

How RSI Confirms Breakout Validity

- A valid breakout is often accompanied by **RSI breaking above 70 (bullish)** or **below 30 (bearish)**.
- Look for **momentum acceleration** on RSI—steep slopes and fast moves support strength.
- Divergence between RSI and price suggests a **lack of conviction** and potential reversal.

Bullish Breakout Confirmation Strategy

- Wait for price to **close above resistance** on strong volume.
- RSI should be breaking out above **60** at the same time.
- Confirm with:
    - Bullish candle close above resistance
    - Volume spike
    - No immediate bearish rejection
- Consider entry on a **pullback to the breakout zone** if RSI stays elevated.

Example:

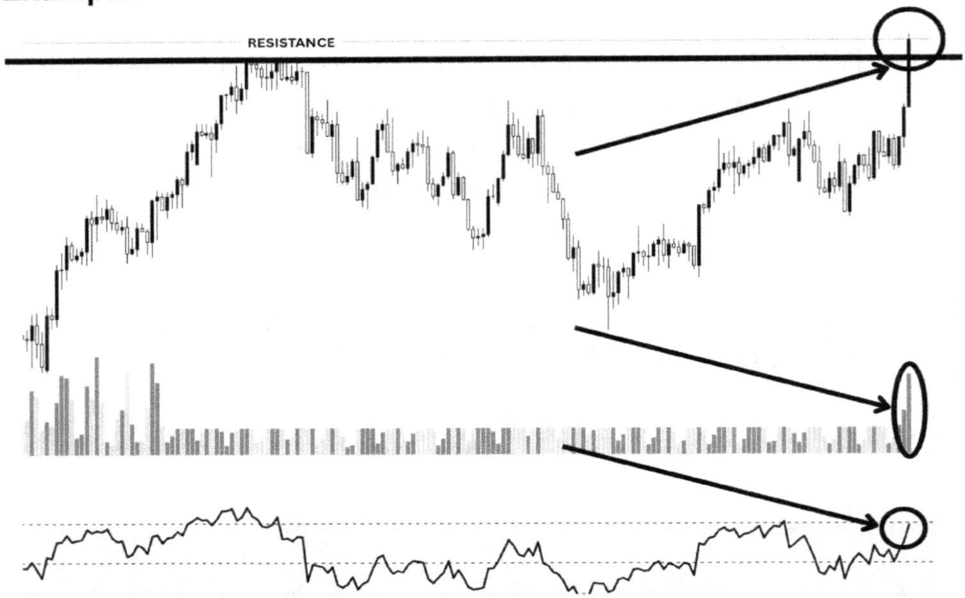

Price closed above the resistance level with a strong bullish candle, along with a spike in volume, and RSI is above 60 confirming the breakout and a possible move higher

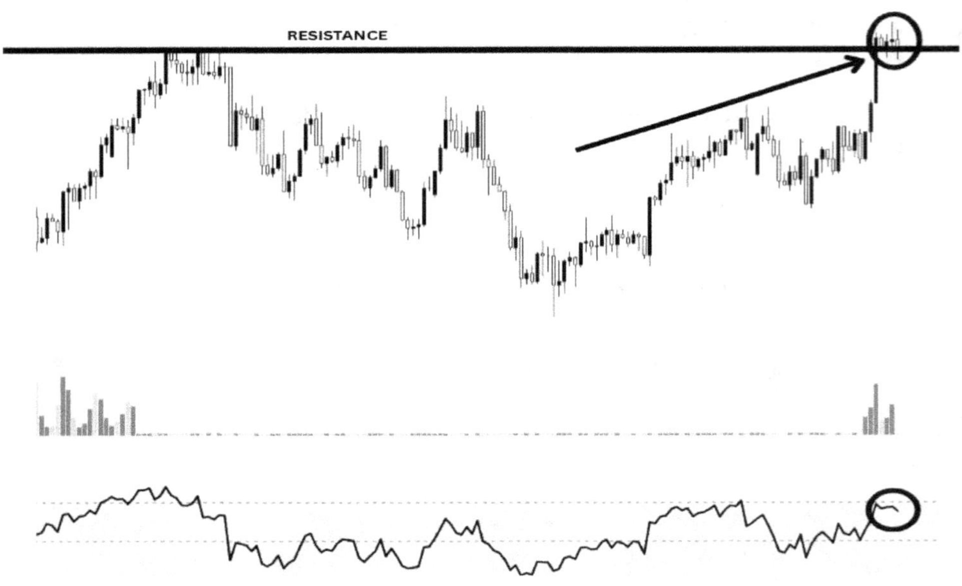

Price pulls back to the breakout zone and RSI is still above 60 confirming the move higher, enter long position as soon as price closes at the breakout zone

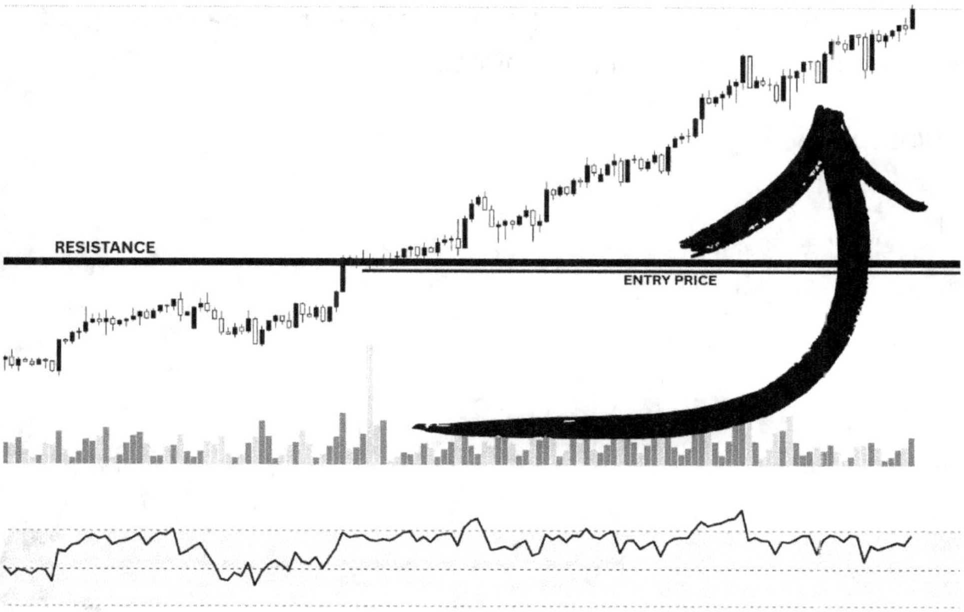

Chart shows a strong move to the upside

Bearish Breakout Confirmation Strategy

- Price breaks and closes below **support** with strong volume.
- RSI should confirm with a move **below 40**, showing strong downside momentum.
- Look for:
    - Bearish candle close below support
    - No immediate bullish rejection
    - Volume supporting the move

- Short entries can be taken on a **retest of broken support**, using RSI to confirm continuation.

Example:

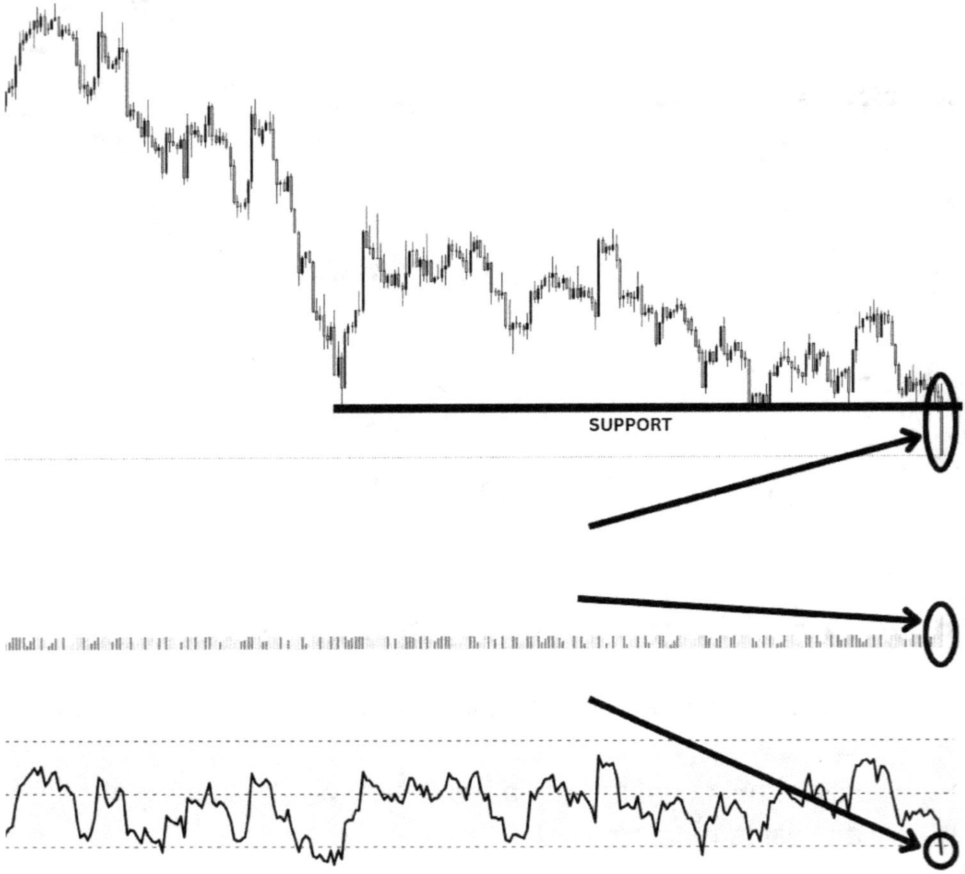

Price closed below the support level with a strong bearish candle, along with a spike in volume, and RSI is below 40 confirming the breakout and a possible move lower

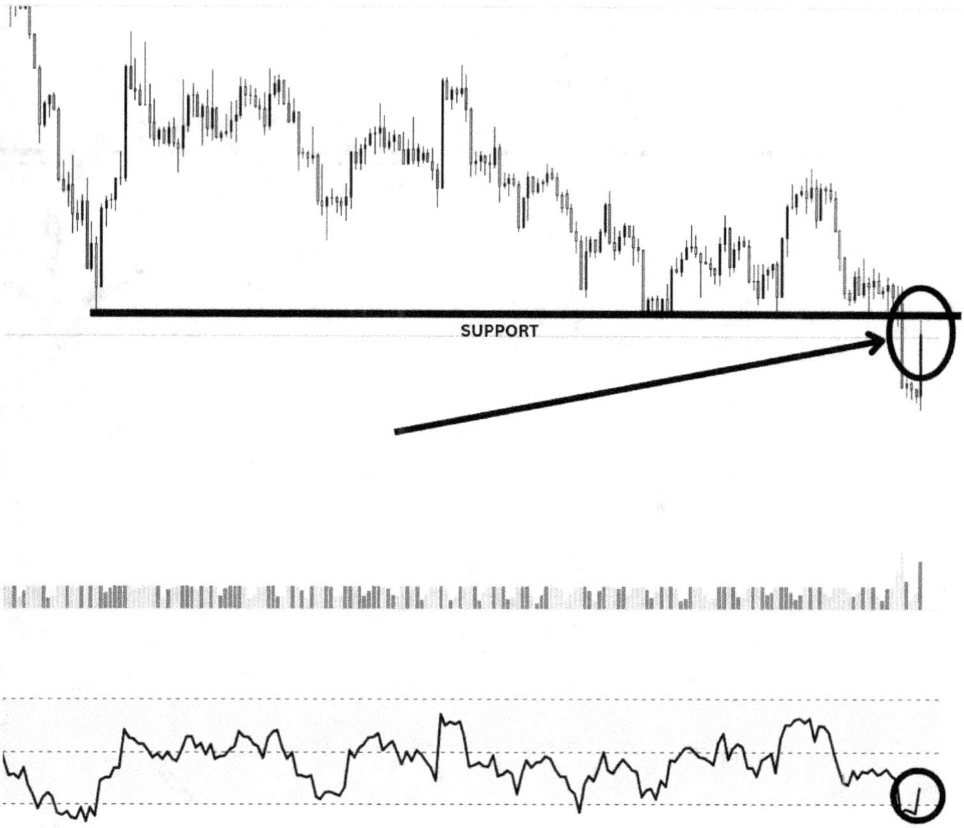

Price pulls back to and retests the support level and RSI is still below 40 confirming the move lower, enter short position as soon as price closes under the support level after retest

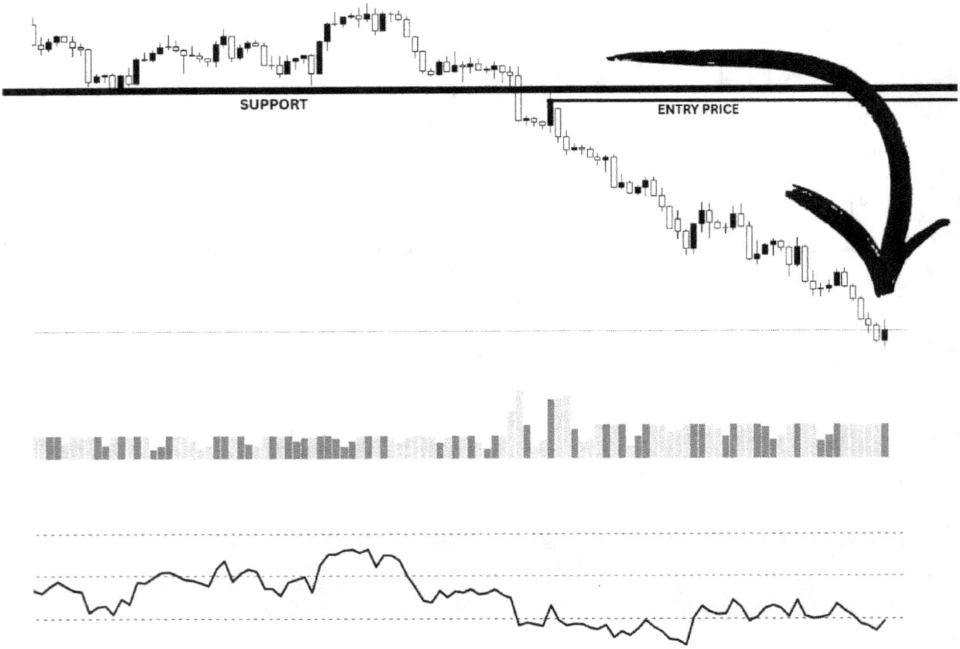

Chart shows a strong move to the downside

Using RSI Divergence to Avoid Traps

- **Bearish divergence** at breakout highs = warning of a potential failed breakout.
- **Bullish divergence** at breakdown lows = trap for bears, likely to reverse.
- Divergence tells you **the breakout is not supported** by real momentum.

How to Use RSI With Other Tools

- Combine RSI with **volume spikes**: both must align for conviction.
- Use RSI in conjunction with **breakout candle patterns**:
    - Marubozu = strong
    - Rejection wicks = weak
- Use **RSI trendlines** to visualize breakout of momentum zones.

How to Avoid Chasing Breakouts Too Late

- If RSI is **already over 80 or under 20**, wait for a pullback—it may be overextended.
- Look for **RSI reset** during the pullback (back to 50 or 60), then re-engage if trend continues.
- Avoid breakout entries when **RSI is flat or indecisive**—you'll likely be entering late.

Summary

Breakouts can bring powerful moves—but they're also full of traps. The RSI is your confirmation tool for separating the **fakeouts from the real trend moves**. When used correctly, RSI helps you determine whether a breakout has the strength to continue or is likely to reverse. Combined with volume and price action, RSI becomes one of the most **reliable filters** to enhance your breakout strategy across any futures market.

Key Takeaways

➤ RSI can confirm breakout strength when it moves **in tandem with price**, breaking above 70 (bullish) or below 30 (bearish).

➤ **Divergence between RSI and price** is a red flag—a likely trap or failed breakout.

➤ Use RSI along with **volume spikes and candle closes** for full breakout confirmation.

➤ Enter breakouts on **pullbacks**, not right at the breakout, if RSI remains strong.

➤ Avoid breakout trades when RSI is **overextended** or flat—it suggests exhaustion or indecision.

Chapter 9

RSI and Candlestick Signals – Precision Entries

Introduction

Combining RSI with candlestick patterns gives traders a powerful edge for **timing high-probability entries**. While RSI tells us about **momentum and potential reversal zones**, candlestick signals confirm **exact moments** of buyer or seller strength. This chapter explores how the synergy of RSI and candlestick patterns can lead to **precise, confident entries** in oil, gold, and index futures markets.

Why RSI Alone Isn't Enough

- RSI tells us when a market is **overbought or oversold**, but not **when to act**.
- Acting on RSI alone can lead to **premature entries** if no price action confirmation exists.
- Candlestick signals **refine the timing** of RSI-based setups.

Benefits of Combining RSI with Candlestick Patterns

- Enhances entry precision by waiting for **clear visual signals** in price structure.
- Reduces false signals and **whipsaws** by requiring **multiple layers of confirmation**.
- Provides confidence for **tight stop-loss placement** under/above the candle signal.

Common Bullish Candle Confirmations:

- **Doji (at support):** Market indecision; potential reversal when found at key levels.

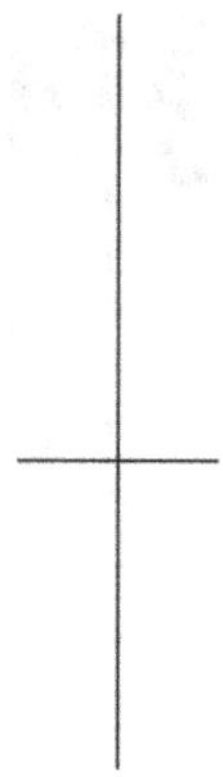

- **Bullish Engulfing:** Large candle "engulfs" the prior one—shows momentum shift.

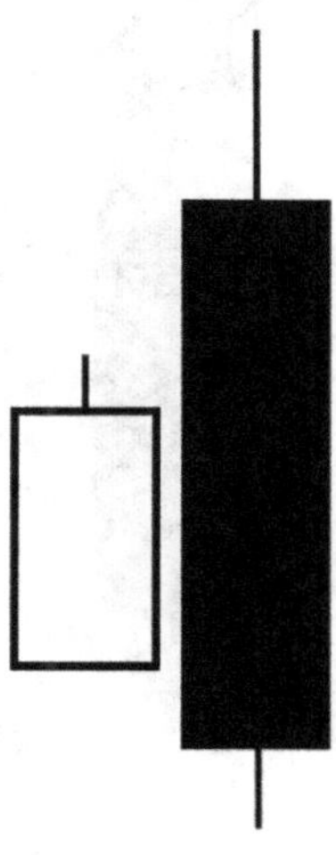

- **Hammer / Pin Bar:** Long wick to the downside signals rejection of a price level.

- **Bullish Marubozu:** Strong momentum with no wicks.

- **Inside Bar Breakout (upward):** Price consolidates—watch for breakout.

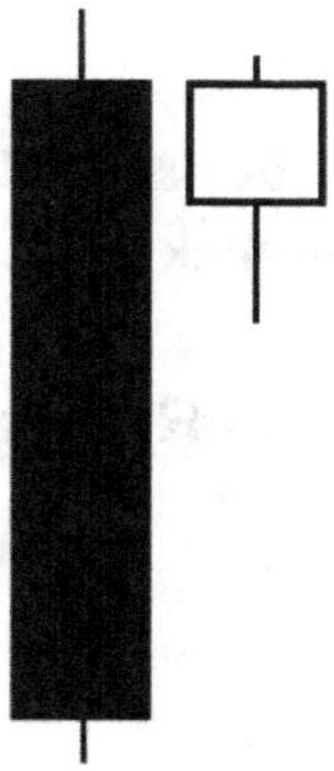

- **Three-Bar Continuation (upward):** Sequence of higher highs and higher lows with volume support.

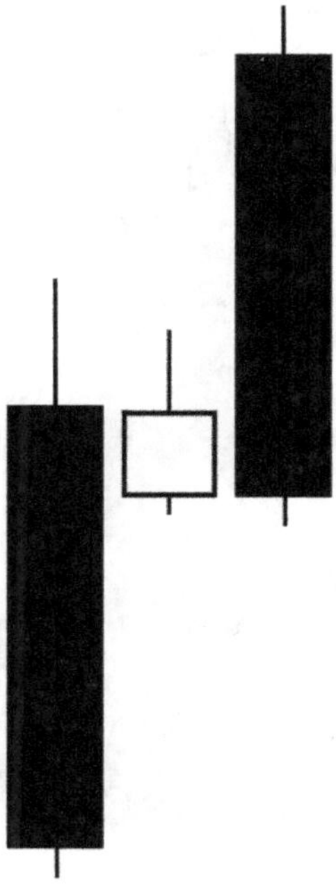

Ideal RSI Zones for Candlestick Confirmation

- **Overbought (>70)** or **Oversold (<30)** zones are primary RSI reversal areas.
- **Mid-level RSI (40–60)** is best for **trend continuation entries** with candlestick patterns.
- Combine **location on RSI** with the **story the candles tell** for best results.

Bullish RSI + Candlestick Entry Setups

- RSI < 30 followed by a **bullish engulfing candle** = strong reversal signal.

Example:

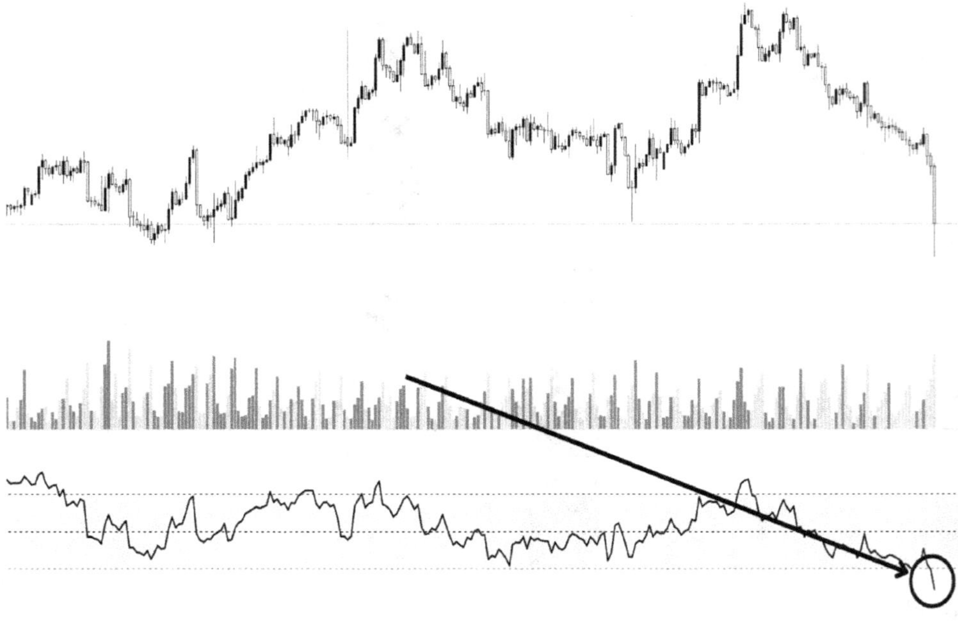

RSI falls below 30

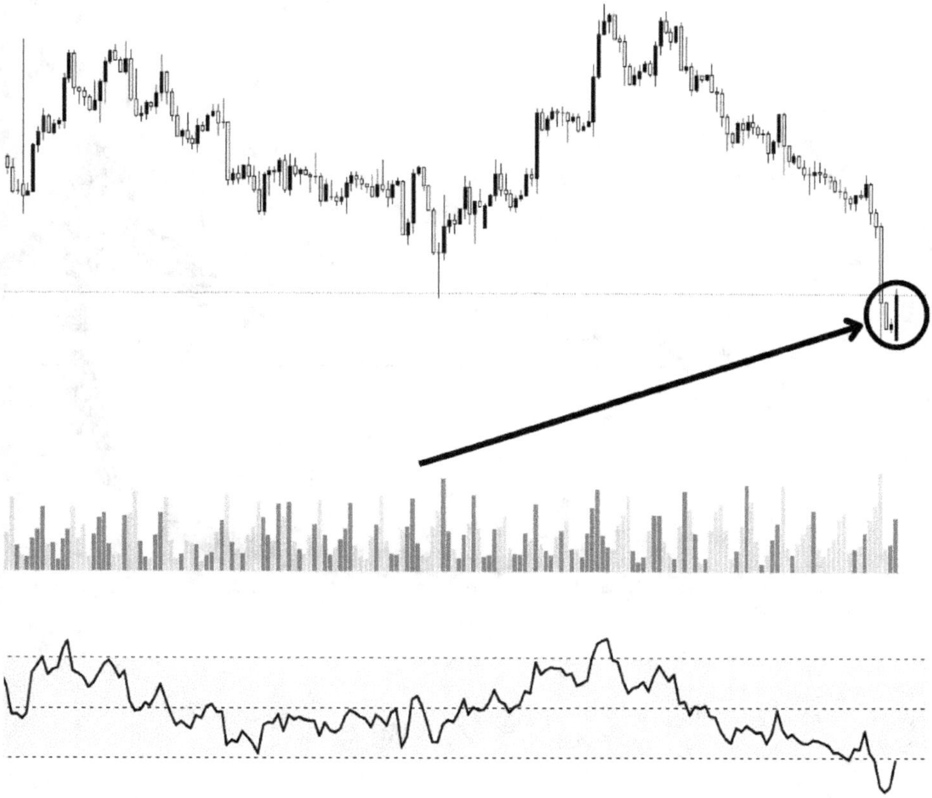

A bullish engulfing candle follows the cross below 30, making it a strong reversal signal and confirming a move to the upside. Enter a long position at the close of the bullish engulfing candle

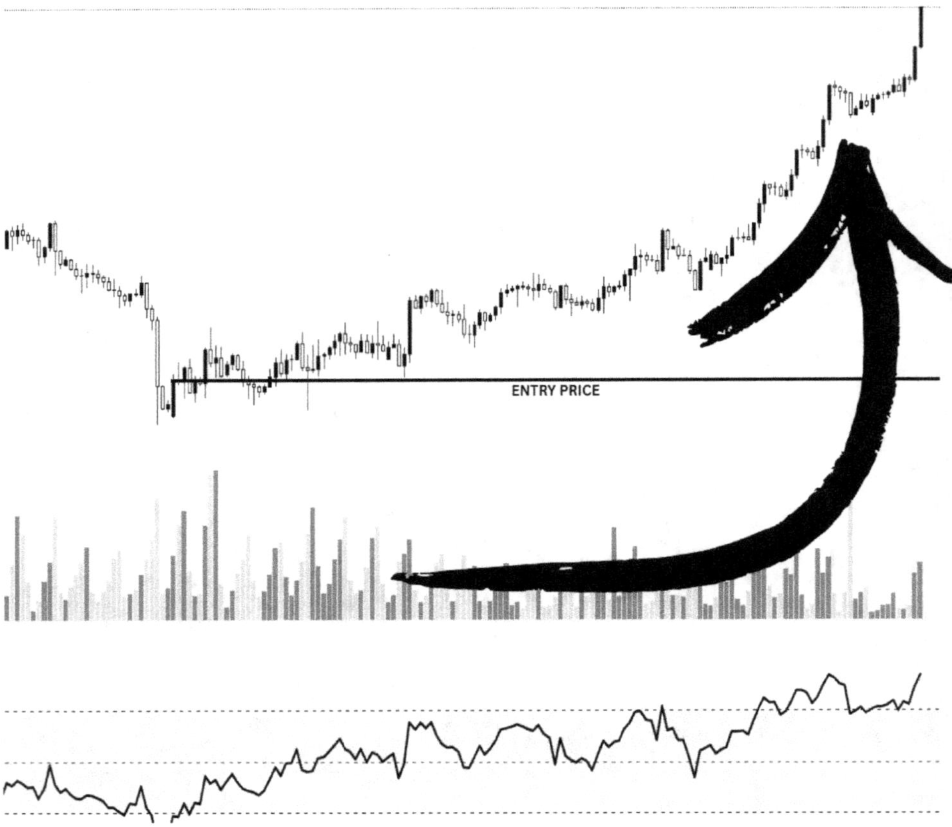

Chart shows a strong move to the upside

- RSI crossing below 30 + **hammer candle** = strong reversal signal.

Example:

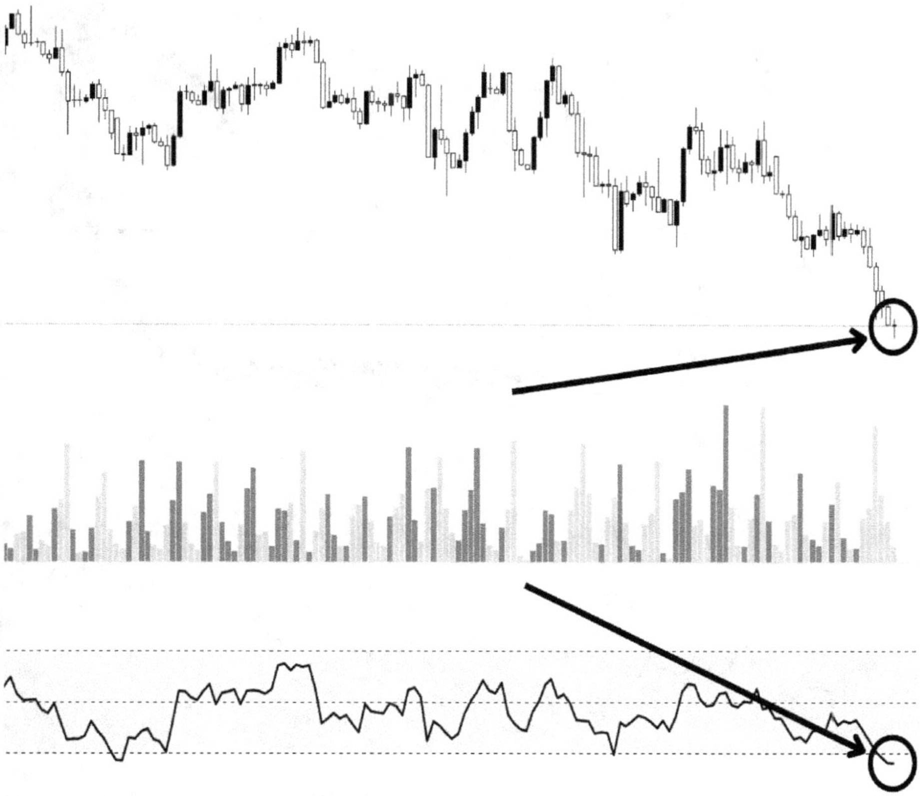

RSI crosses below 30 with a hammer candle, making it a strong reversal signal and confirming a move to the upside. Enter a long position at the close of the hammer candle

Chart shows a strong move to the upside

Common Bearish Candle Confirmations:

- **Doji (at resistance):** Market indecision; potential reversal when found at key levels.

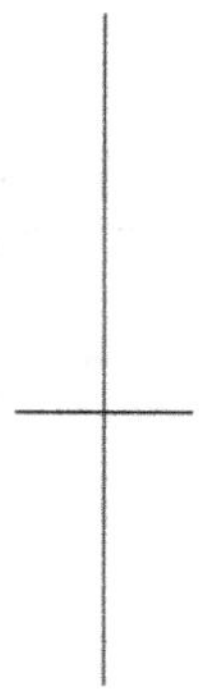

- **Bearish Engulfing:** Large candle "engulfs" the prior one—shows momentum shift.

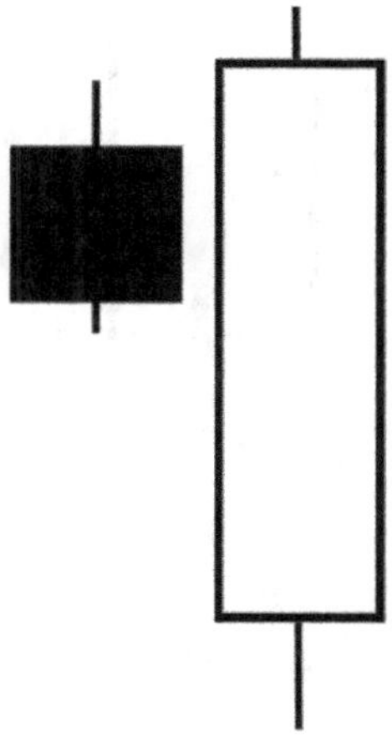

- **Shooting Star / Inverted Hammer:** Long wick to the upside signals rejection of a price level.

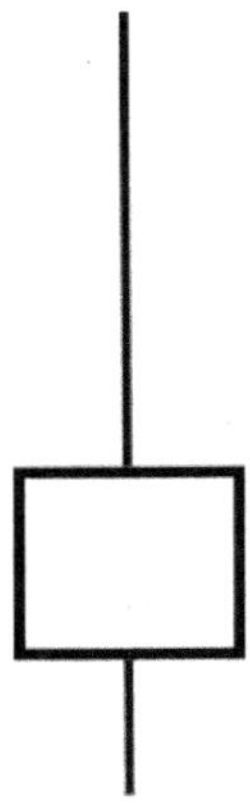

- **Bearish Marubozu:** Strong momentum with no wicks.

- **Inside Bar Breakout (downward):** Price consolidates, watch for breakout.

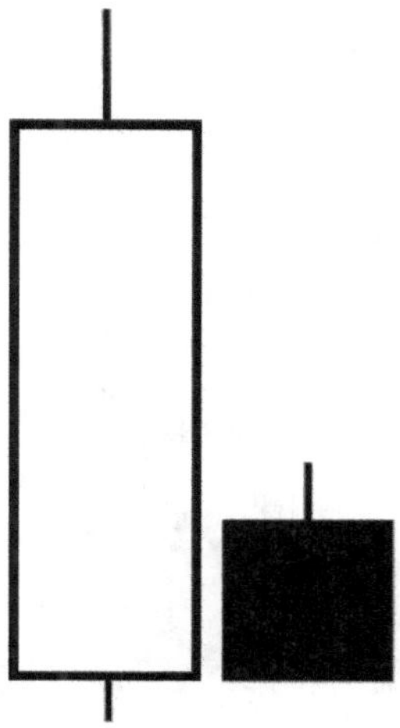

- **Three-Bar Continuation (downward):** Sequence of lower highs and lower lows with volume support.

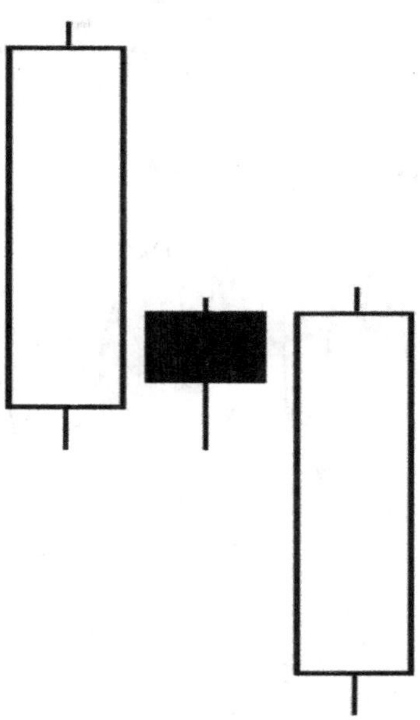

Bearish RSI + Candlestick Entry Setups

- RSI > 70 followed by a **bearish engulfing candle** = strong reversal signal.

Example:

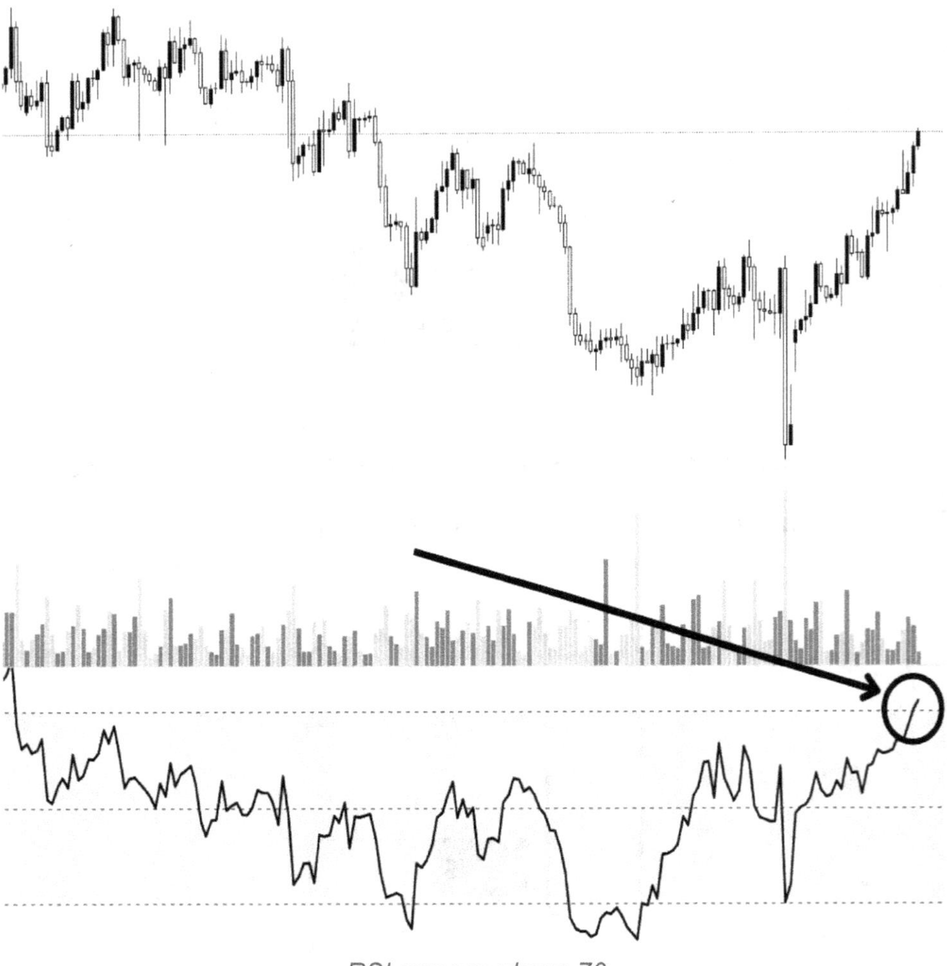

RSI crosses above 70

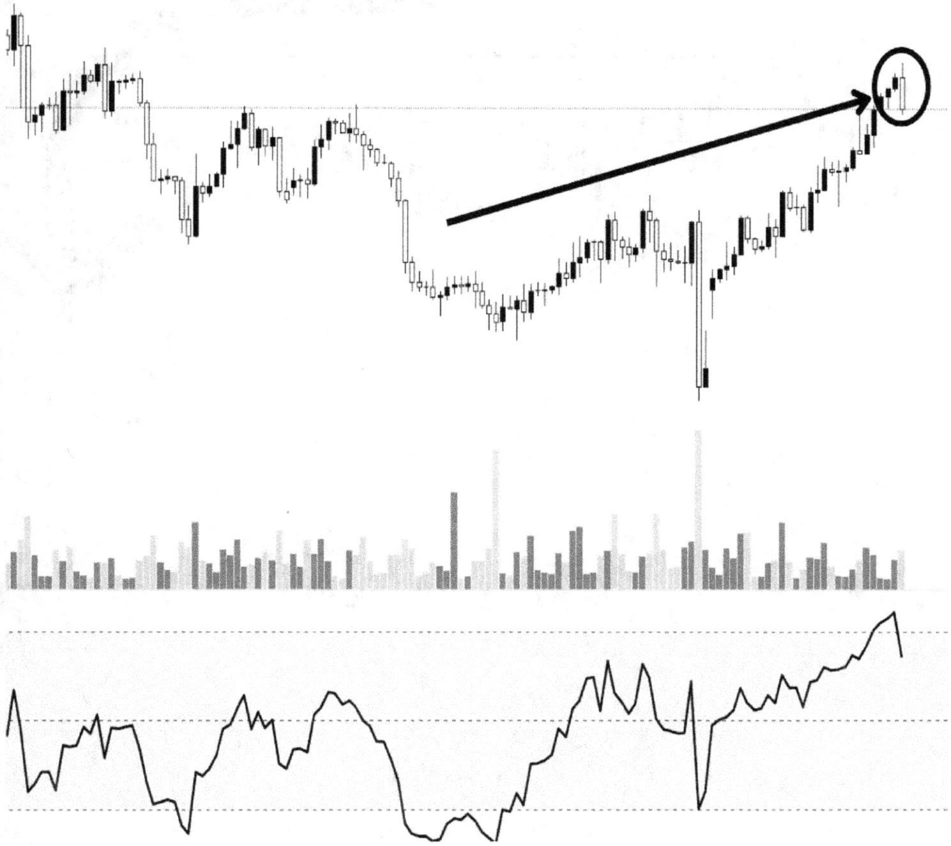

A bearish engulfing candle follows the cross above 70, making it a strong reversal signal and confirming a move to the downside. Enter a short position at the close of the bearish engulfing candle

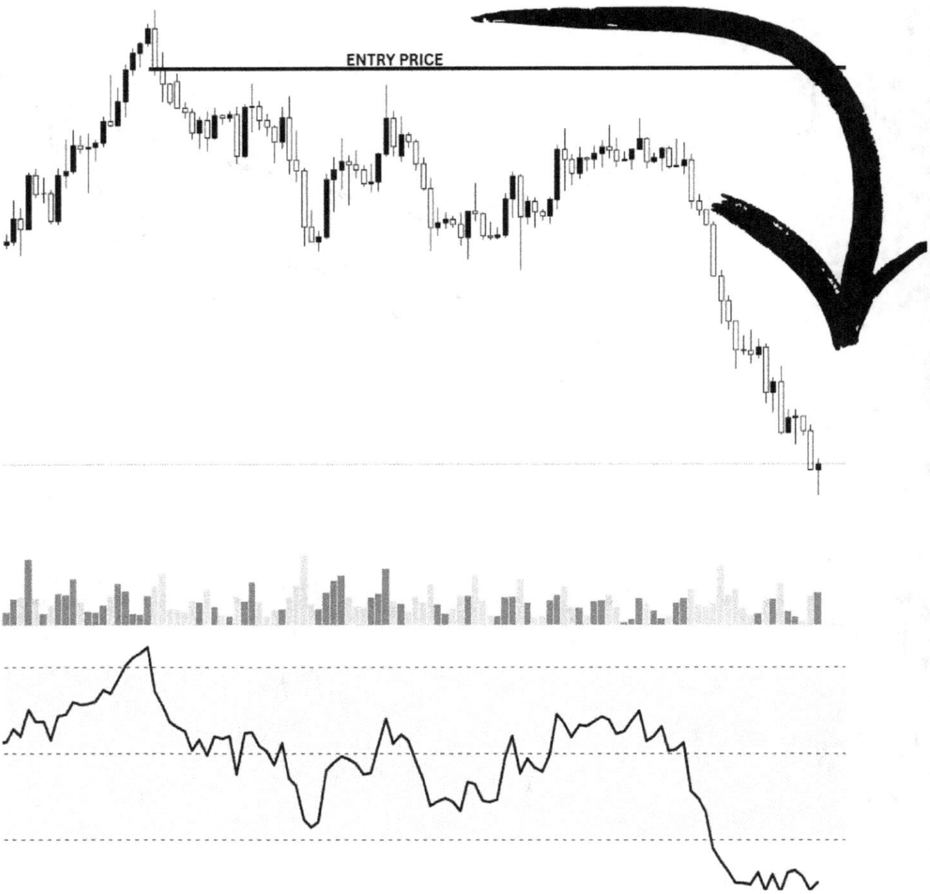

Chart shows a strong move to the downside

- RSI crossing above 70 + **shooting star** = strong reversal signal.

Example:

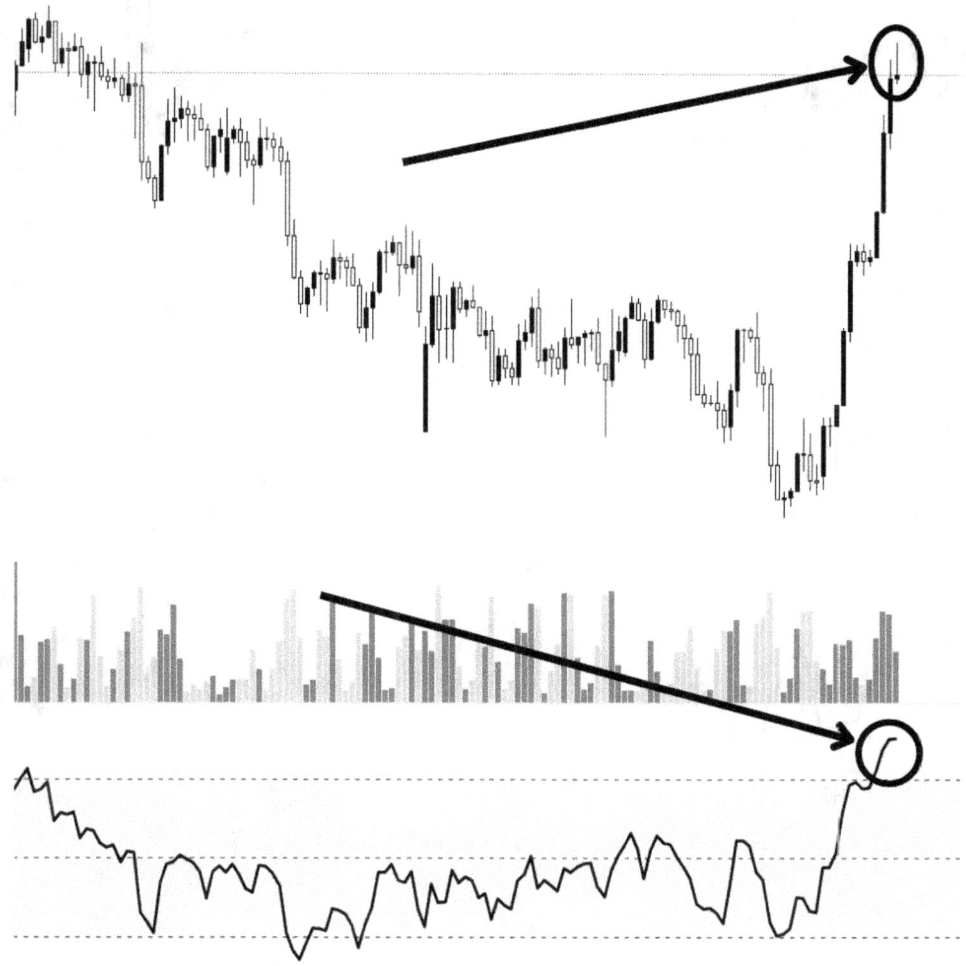

RSI crosses above 70 with a shooting star candle, making it a strong reversal signal and confirming a move to the downside. Enter a short position at the close of the shooting star candle

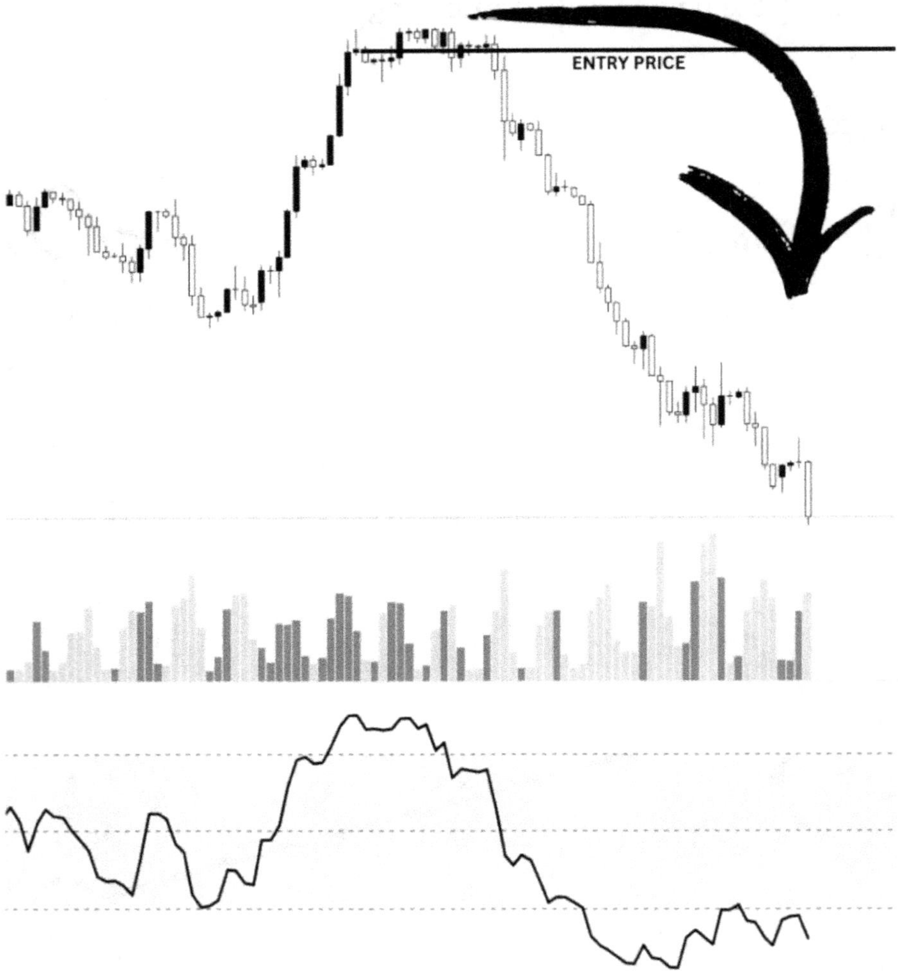

Chart shows a strong move to the downside

- Combine RSI + candlestick entries with **trend direction** for high accuracy.

How to Structure the Trade

- **Entry**: After a confirmation candle closes after a break above 70 (bearish) or a break below 30 (bullish).
- **Stop Loss**: Just below candle low (bullish) or above candle high (bearish).
- **Take Profit Target**: Based on recent swing levels or when RSI crosses above 70 (bullish) or crosses below 30 (bearish).

Example (bullish):

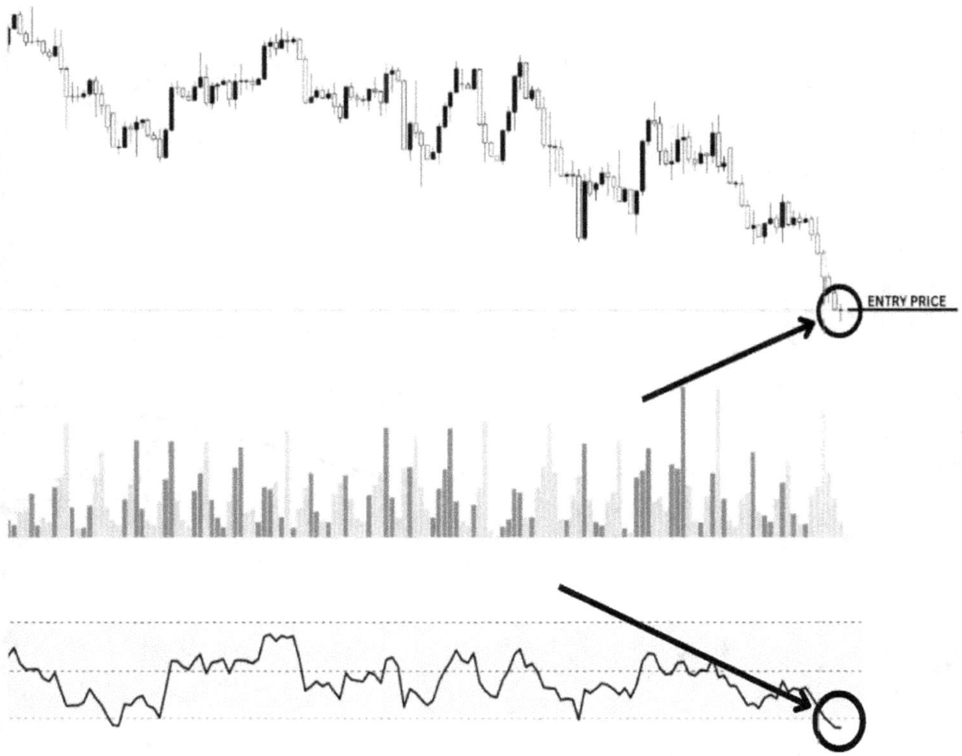

RSI falls below 30 followed by a hammer candle, making it a strong reversal signal and confirming a move to the upside. Enter a long position at the close of the hammer candle

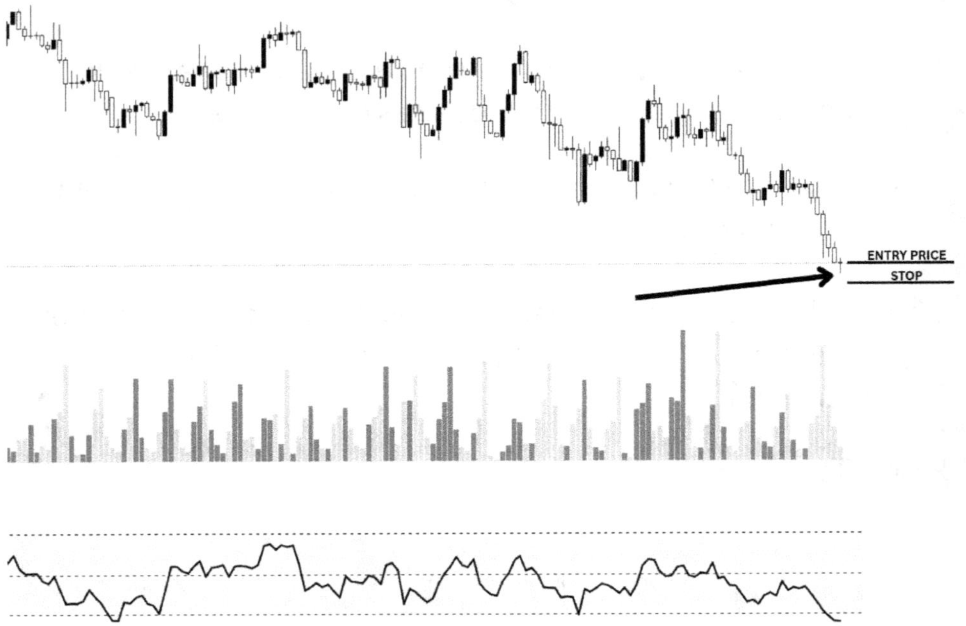

Set stop loss to just below the hammer candle low

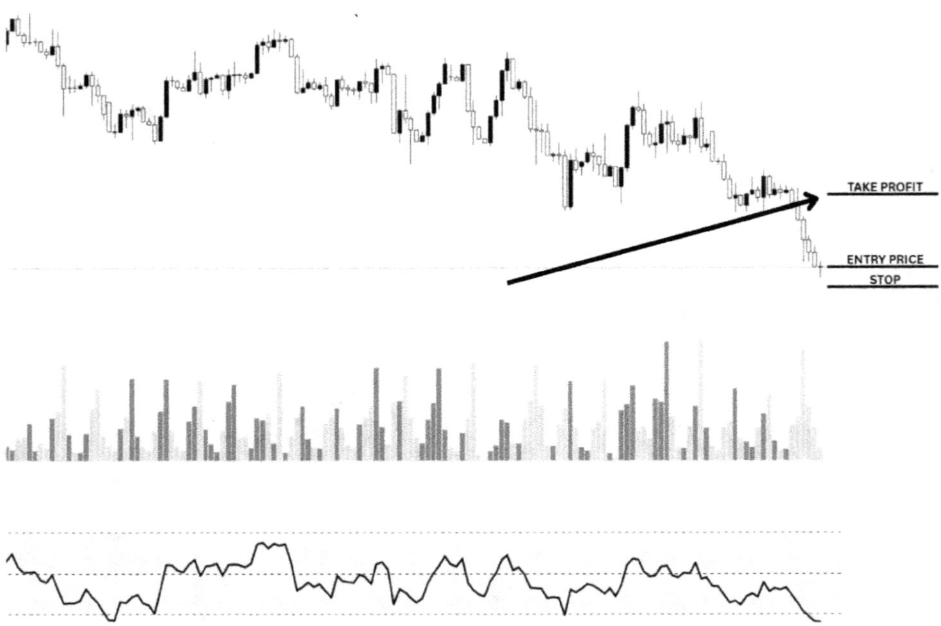

Set take profit to the most recent swing level

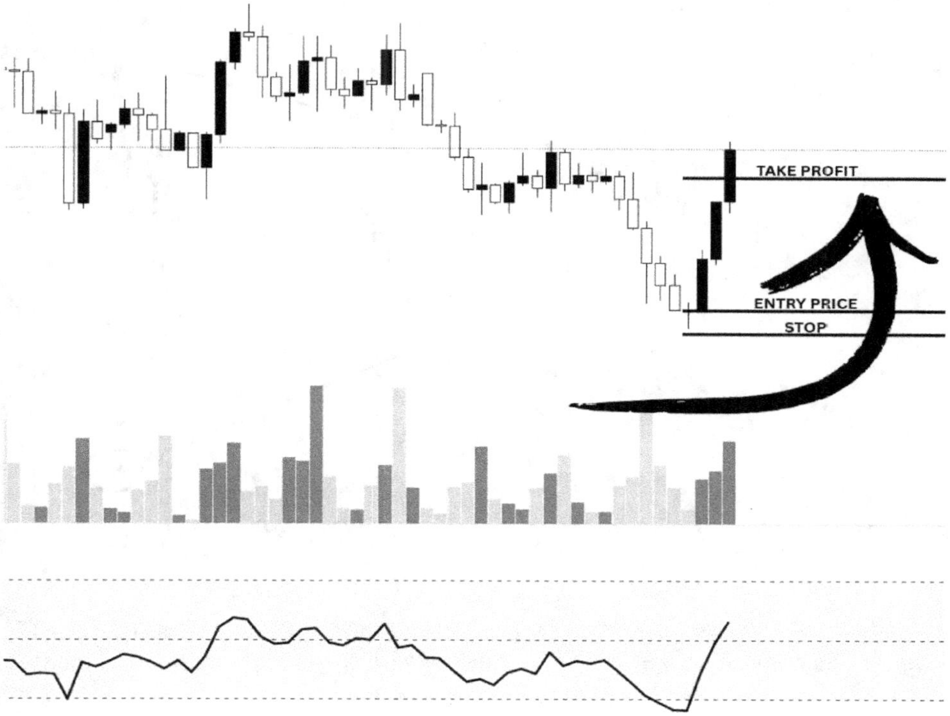

Chart shows a strong move to the upside while hitting the take profit target

Example (bearish):

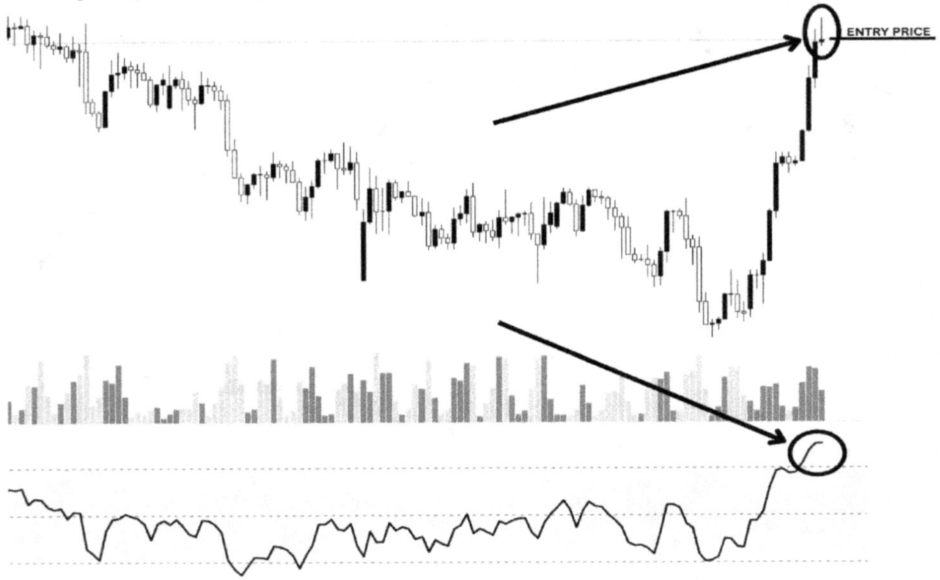

RSI crosses above 70 with a shooting star candle, making it a strong reversal signal and confirming a move to the downside. Enter a short position at the close of the shooting star candle

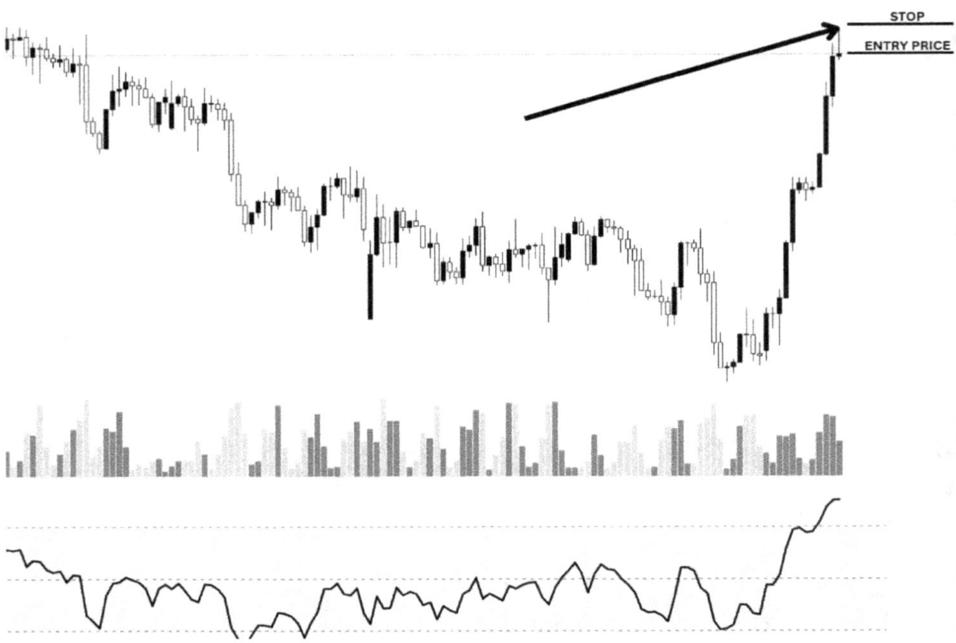

Set stop loss to just above the shooting star candle high

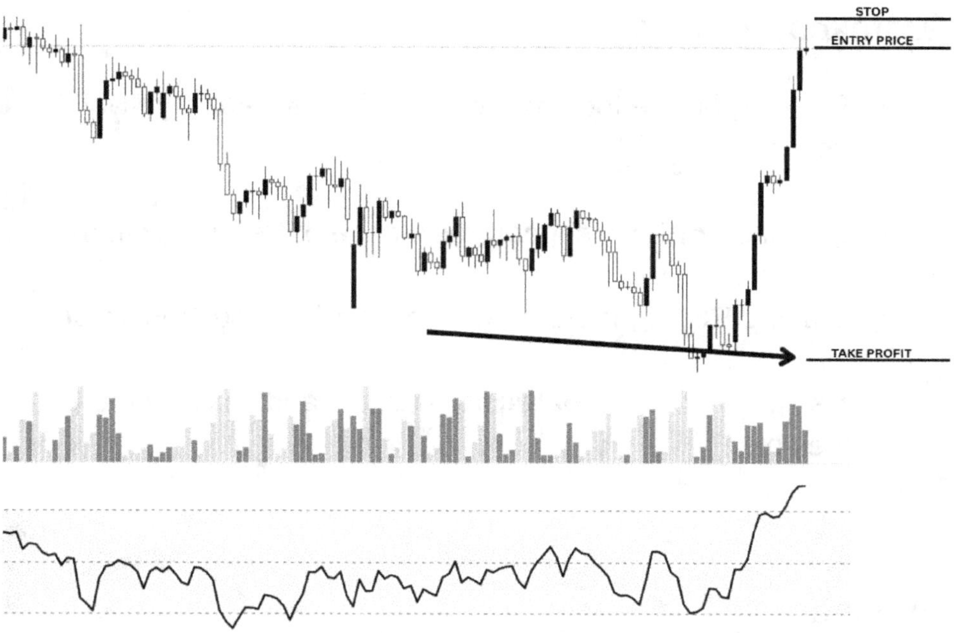

Set take profit to the most recent swing level

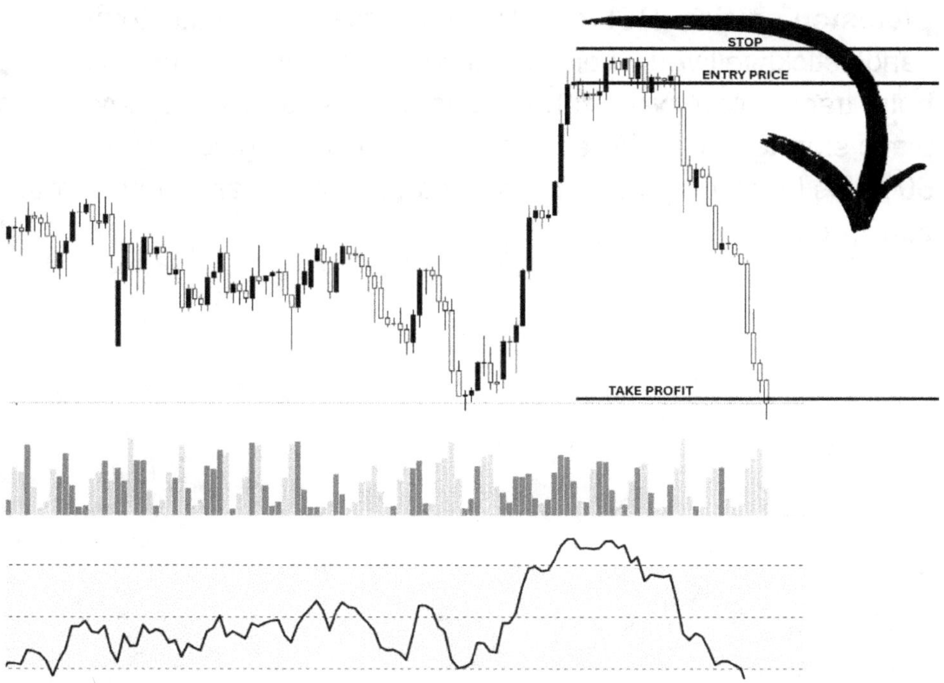

Chart shows a strong move to the downside while hitting the take profit target

Mistakes to Avoid

- Entering before the **candlestick closes** — always wait for confirmation.
- Ignoring **context** (support/resistance or trend direction).
- Trading RSI signals in a **strong trend** without confirmation.
- Using **tiny candle patterns**—larger candles carry more weight.

Summary

Pairing RSI with candlestick patterns unlocks a **powerful edge for precision entries**. RSI reveals when a market is ready to turn, and candlesticks tell you when it's actually happening. By combining both, traders can **avoid false signals, enter at optimal levels**, and place smarter stops. Whether you're trading oil, gold, or the S&P 500, this layered approach sharpens your timing and boosts your confidence in every trade.

Key Takeaways

➢ RSI identifies high-probability zones, while candlestick signals define **exact entry points**.

➢ Use **bullish engulfing, hammers, and inside bars** in oversold RSI zones for long entries.

➢ Use **bearish engulfing, shooting stars, and evening stars** in overbought RSI zones for short entries.

➢ Combine RSI divergence with candle confirmation to **boost reversal accuracy**.

➢ Always wait for **candle close**, trade in context, and use tight, logical stop placement.

Chapter 10

RSI and Multi-Timeframe Analysis

Introduction

Successful traders rarely rely on just one chart. Instead, they observe **multiple timeframes** to get a deeper understanding of market structure, momentum, and key inflection points. In this chapter, you'll learn how to apply the **Relative Strength Index (RSI)** in a multi-timeframe setup to increase your trade accuracy, improve entry timing, and avoid false signals—especially across oil, gold, and index futures.

Why Use Multi-Timeframe RSI?

- Each timeframe reveals a **different layer of market psychology**.
- Combining RSI readings from higher and lower timeframes adds **context and confirmation** to your trades.
- Helps you align short-term trades with **larger trend direction**.
- Filters out **choppy or misleading signals** on the smaller timeframe when the larger trend is still intact.

Choosing Your Timeframes

- Use a **3-to-1 ratio** between timeframes for layered RSI analysis:
    - 5-min + 15-min
    - 15-min + 1-hr
    - 1-hr + 4-hr
- For day traders:
    - **Lower timeframe (LTF):** entry and precision
    - **Higher timeframe (HTF):** trend context and filter

HTF RSI Sets the Bias, LTF RSI Times the Entry

- Think of the higher timeframe RSI as your **weather forecast**—it sets the tone.
- The lower timeframe RSI is your **minute-by-minute radar**—it tells you when to open the umbrella.

Trading Long: Bullish RSI Stack

- HTF RSI is **above 50**, preferably heading toward 60 or 70 = trend is strong.
- Wait for LTF RSI to:
    - Dip into an **oversold level** (below 30)
    - Form a bullish candlestick pattern or divergence
- Enter long once LTF RSI confirms momentum shift upward.

Example:

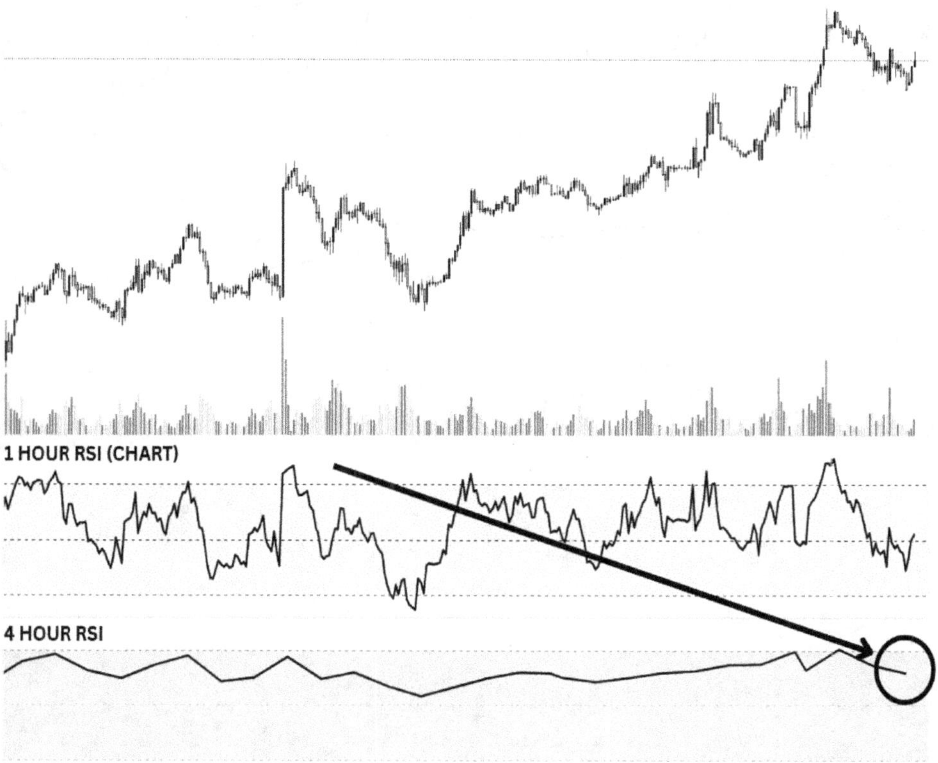

The higher time frame RSI (4 hour) is above 50, confirming a strong uptrend

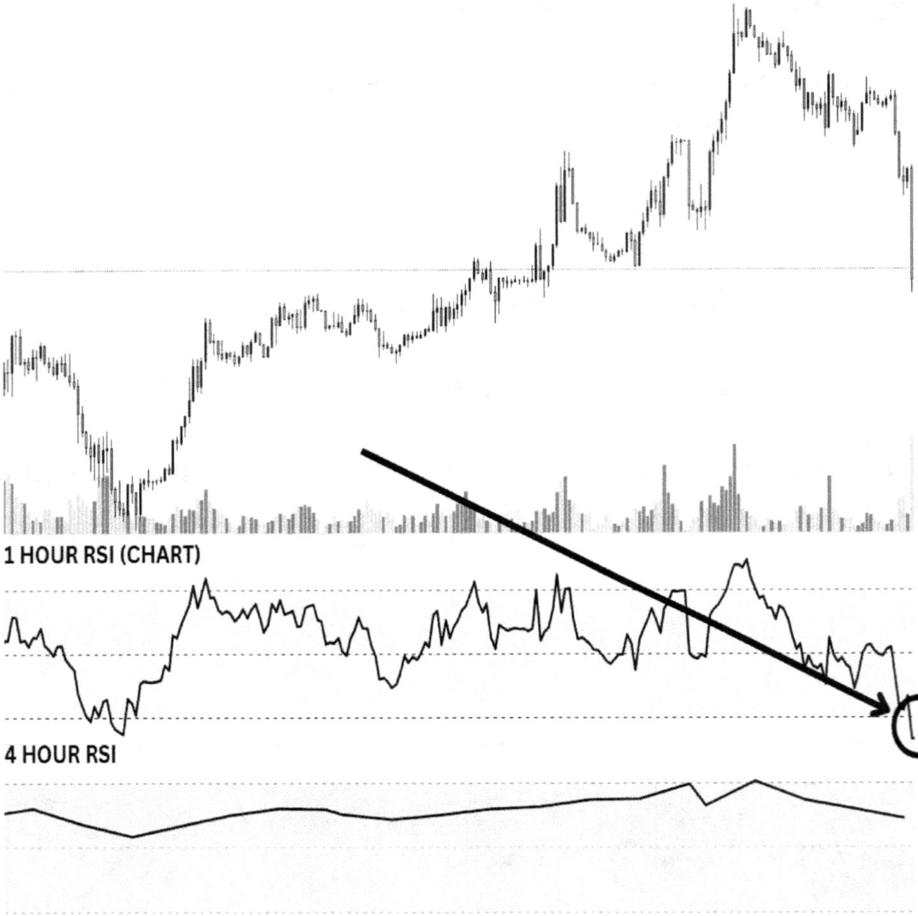

The lower time frame RSI (1 hour) falls below 30, signaling price is oversold and a potential upside reversal

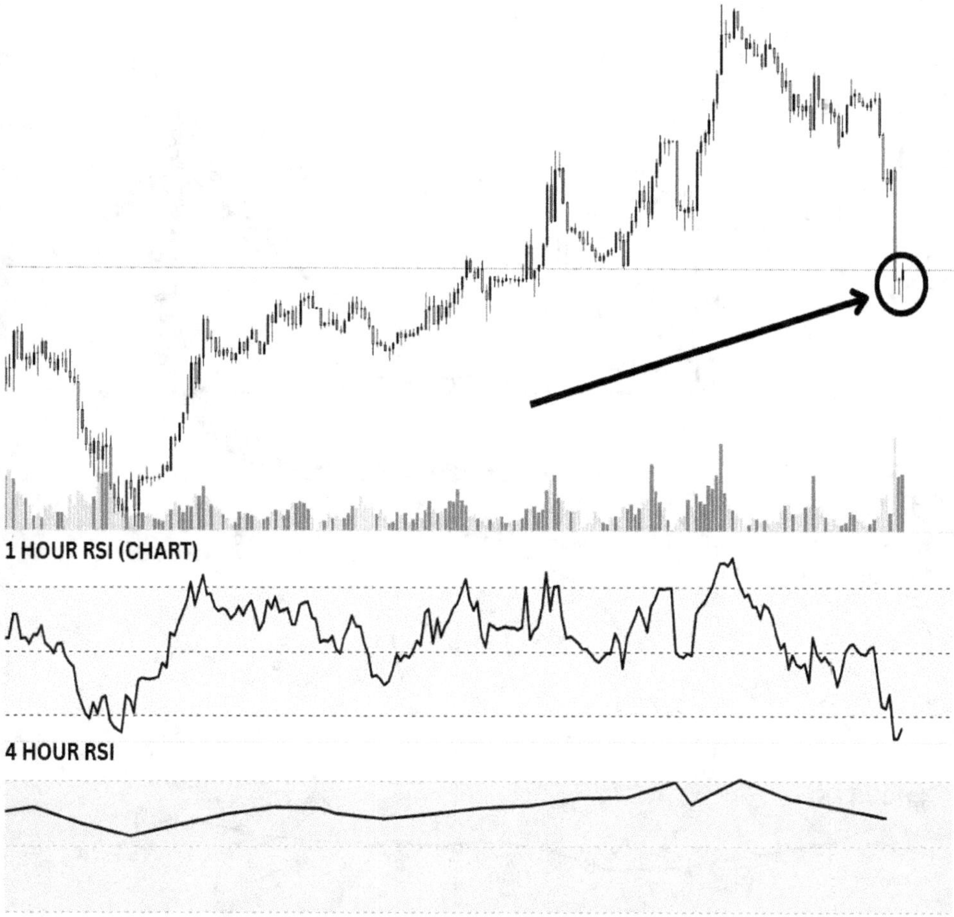

A bullish engulfing candle following the dip below 30 on the lower time frame RSI (1 hour) confirms the move to the upside, enter a long position at the close of the bullish engulfing candle

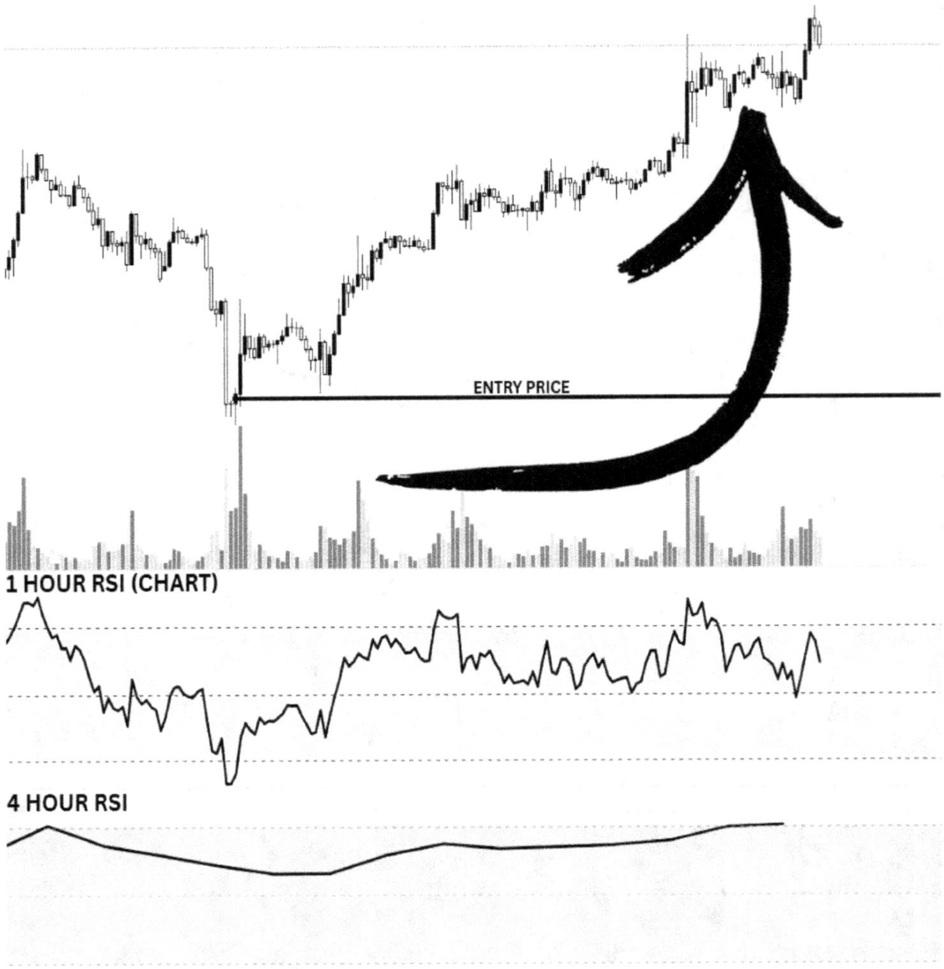

Chart shows a strong move to the upside

Trading Short: Bearish RSI Stack

- HTF RSI is **below 50**, ideally pressing toward 30.
- Look for LTF RSI to:
    - Spike up to an overbought level (above 70)
    - Show a bearish candlestick pattern or divergence

Example:

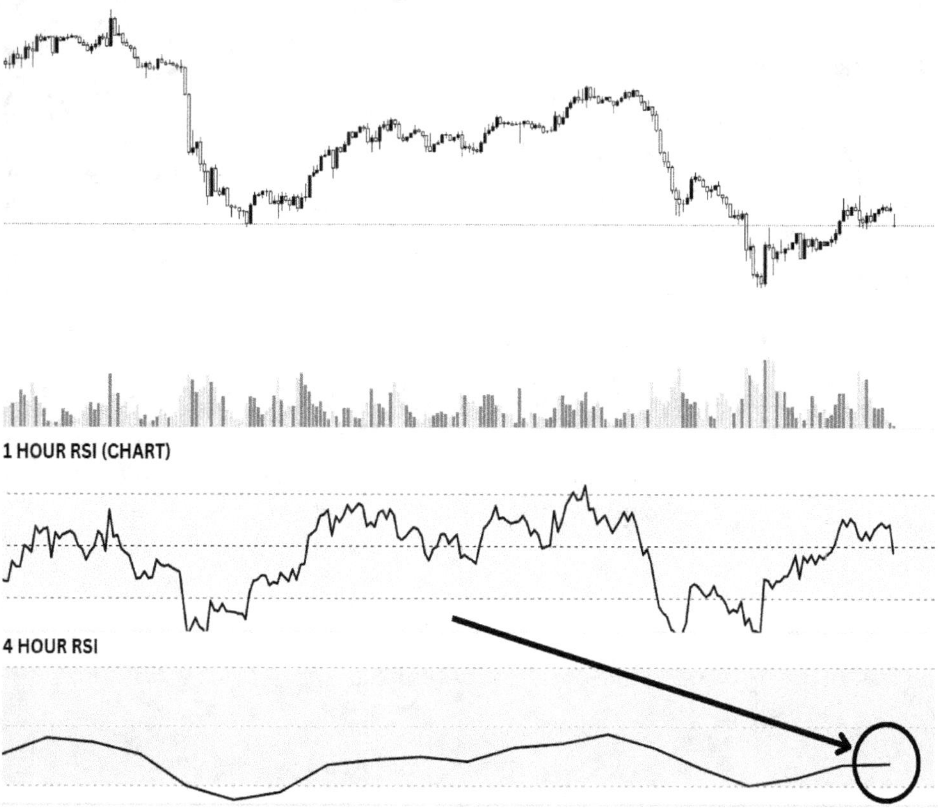

The higher time frame RSI (4 hour) is below 50, confirming a strong downtrend

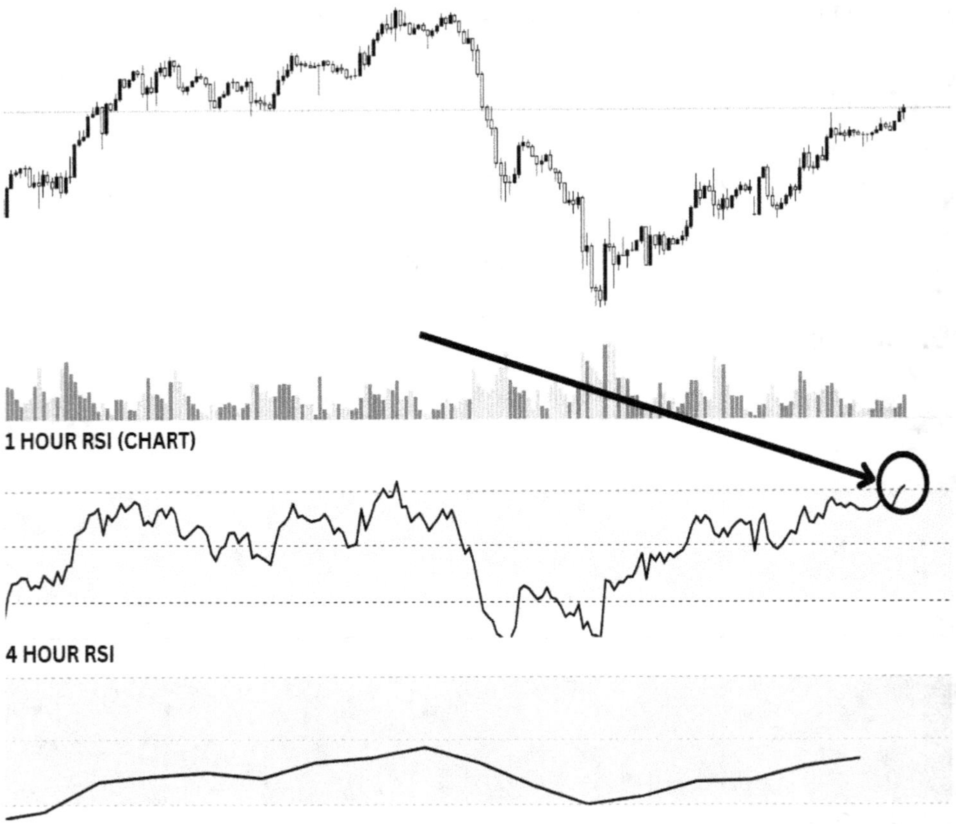

The lower time frame RSI (1 hour) crosses above 70, signaling price is overbought and a potential downside reversal

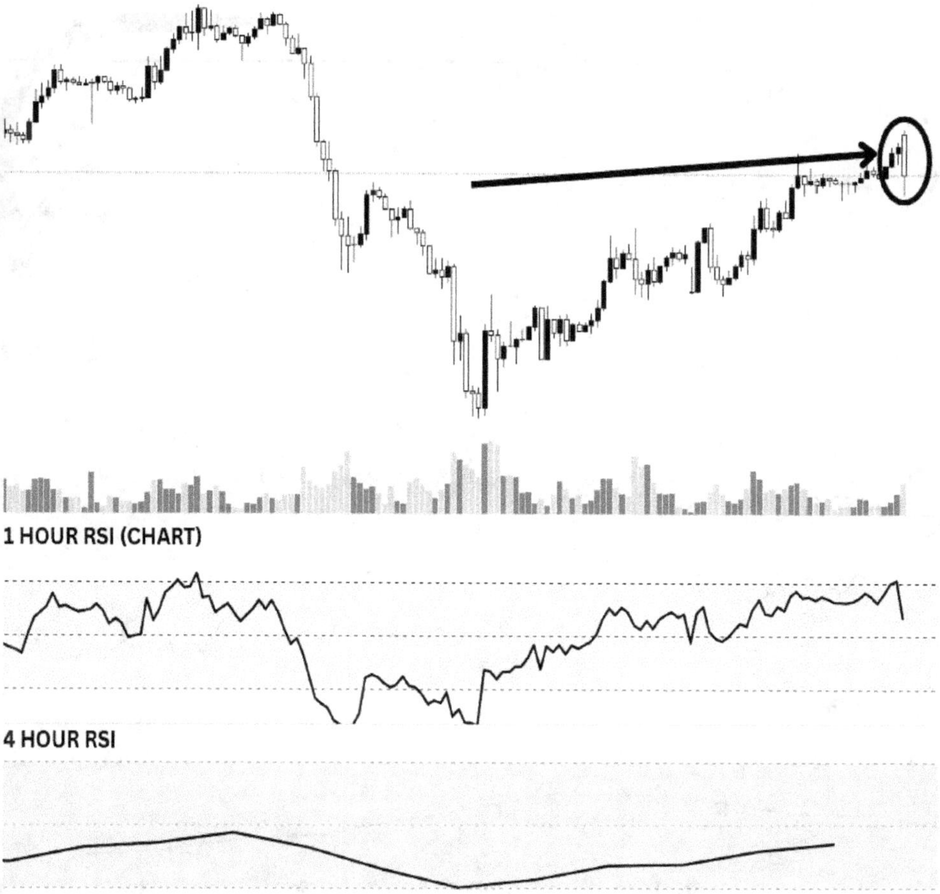

A bearish engulfing candle following the cross above 70 on the lower time frame RSI (1 hour) confirms the move to the downside, enter a short position at the close of the bearish engulfing candle

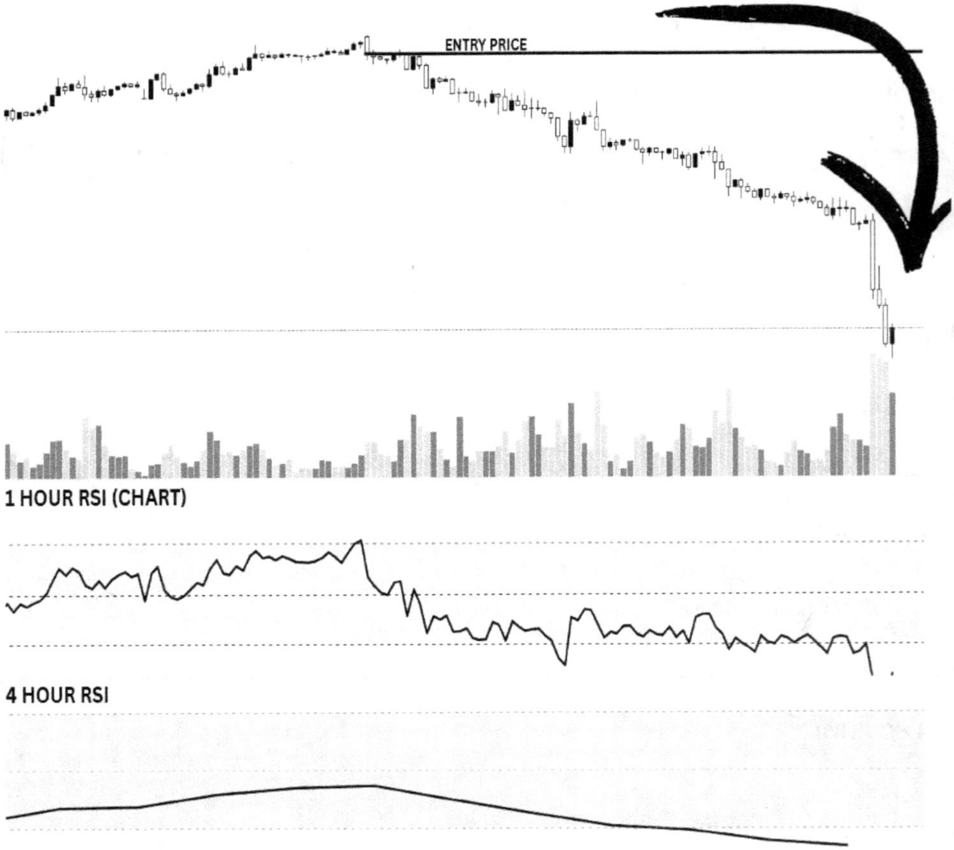

Chart shows a strong move to the downside

Multi TImeframe RSI works Great for:

- **Index futures** during consolidation phases
- **Gold** before macro catalyst events
- **Oil** on inventory report days

Timeframe Conflicts: When RSI Disagrees

- Occasionally, HTF and LTF RSI will **contradict each other**:
    - HTF is overbought (RSI 70+), but LTF gives buy signal.
    - LTF is oversold, but HTF is breaking down.
- When in doubt:
    - **Favor the higher timeframe** for trend direction.
    - **Tighten risk** or reduce position size when signals conflict.

Tools & Platforms That Help

- **TradingView:** Excellent for layering multiple RSI indicators
- **ThinkorSwim:** Built-in custom scripts for multi-timeframe indicators
- **NinjaTrader / MetaTrader:** Great for futures traders who want automation

Common Mistakes to Avoid

- Don't enter **against HTF RSI** unless you're scalping and extremely nimble.
- Avoid forcing trades when HTF RSI is in **"decision zones"** (e.g., stuck around 50).
- Don't skip chart structure—RSI must always be used in conjunction with **support/resistance or candlesticks**.

Summary

RSI becomes significantly more powerful when used across **multiple timeframes**. Aligning your short-term trades with the trend direction of a higher timeframe can dramatically improve your win rate, entry timing, and confidence. Whether you're trading oil, gold, or index futures, combining RSI readings across charts is like **adding night vision to your scope—it reveals what others can't see**.

Key Takeaways

➢ Use RSI on multiple timeframes to align trades with larger trends.

➢ HTF RSI shows the trend bias; LTF RSI gives precise entries.

➢ Stack RSI confirmation across timeframes to improve trade confidence.

➢ Favor higher timeframe RSI when signals conflict—don't trade against the trend.

➢ Platforms like TradingView and ThinkorSwim support multi-timeframe RSI overlays.

Chapter 11

RSI and Volume – Uncovering Hidden Strength

Introduction

While RSI helps you spot momentum shifts and overbought/oversold conditions, **volume reveals the strength behind those moves**. When paired together, RSI and volume provide a powerful combination for confirming price direction, identifying exhaustion, and detecting hidden accumulation or distribution. In this chapter, you'll learn how to **use RSI and volume together** to uncover hidden strength—or weakness—in futures markets.

Why Combine RSI with Volume?

- RSI tells you **how stretched momentum is**
- Volume tells you **how committed traders are**
- When RSI signals a move **and volume confirms**, confidence increases
- When RSI shows divergence but volume **spikes in the opposite direction**, it signals manipulation or smart money activity

RSI Moves Mean More with Volume Confirmation

- A **bullish RSI breakout** above 50 is more valid if accompanied by **strong volume**
- A **bearish RSI drop** below 50 is more meaningful with **increased selling volume**
- Volume validates RSI moves by showing that **real capital** is behind the price shift

Volume Spikes with Flat RSI = Trap Setup

- If RSI stays flat while **volume spikes**, the market is likely:
    - Absorbing liquidity (accumulation/distribution)
    - Trapping breakout traders
- Pay close attention when **RSI doesn't confirm** the volume-driven price move

Example:

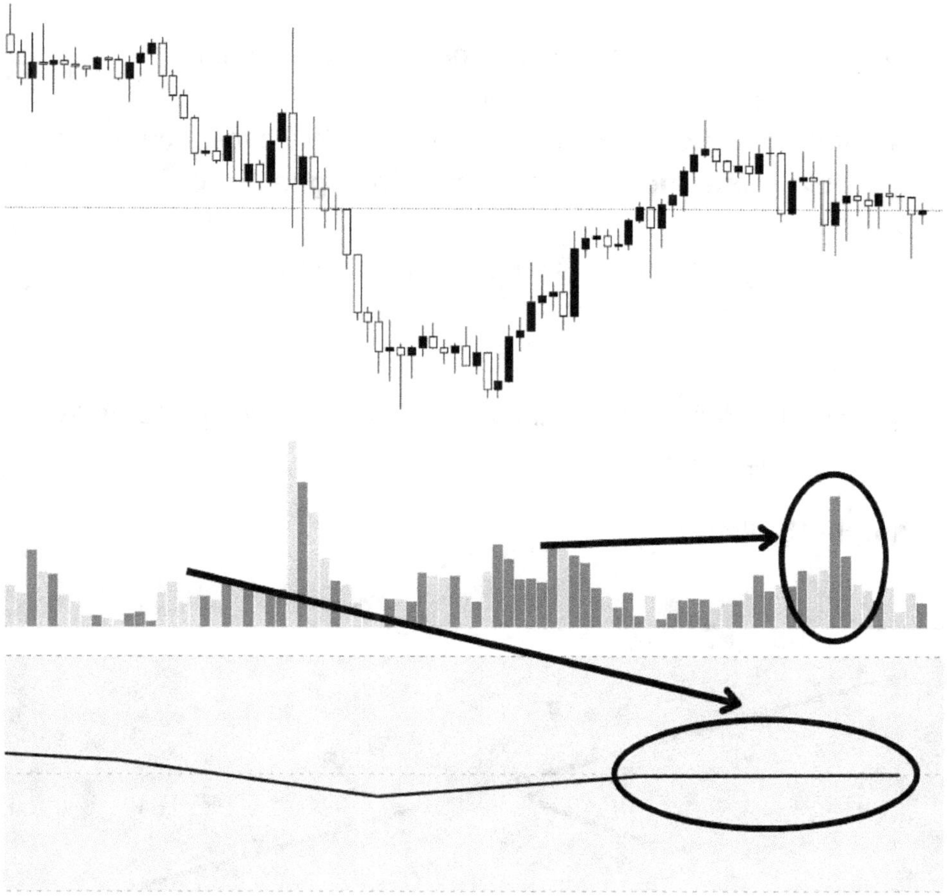

RSI staying flat during volume spikes, signals that the market is absorbing liquidity

RSI Divergence + Volume = Powerful Reversal Signal

- RSI divergence shows **momentum weakness**
- Volume spikes at divergence high or low shows **climactic buying/selling,** confirming a move higher/lower
- Together, this signals a potential **reversal**

- Enter positions on bullish/bearish candlestick patterns for precision entries

Example (bullish):

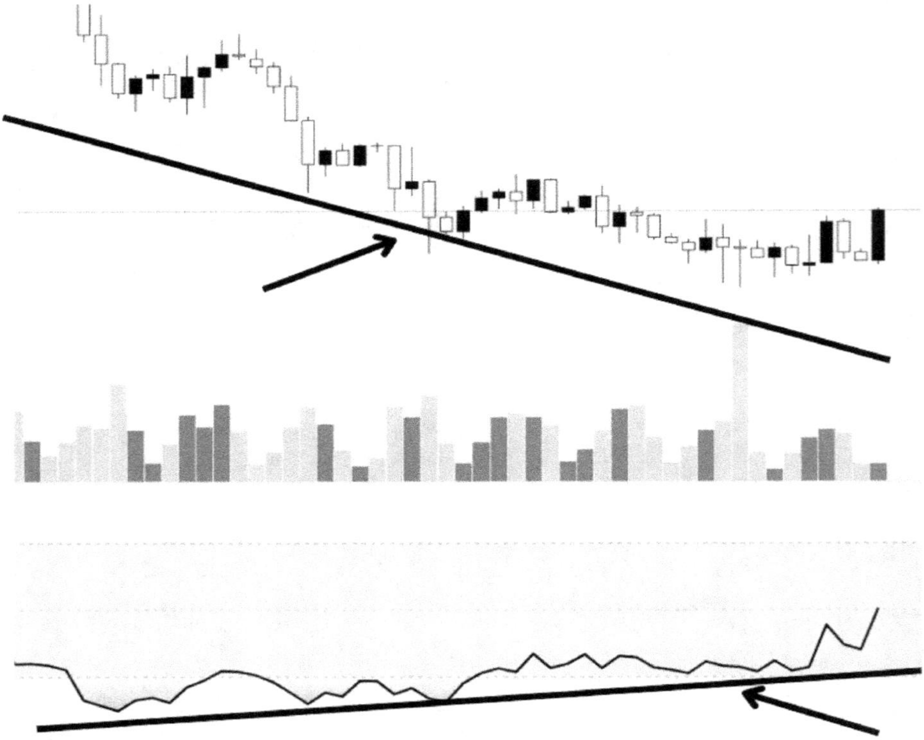

Price is making lower lows and lower highs, but RSI is making higher highs and higher lows, signaling momentum is weak and a possible reversal to the upside

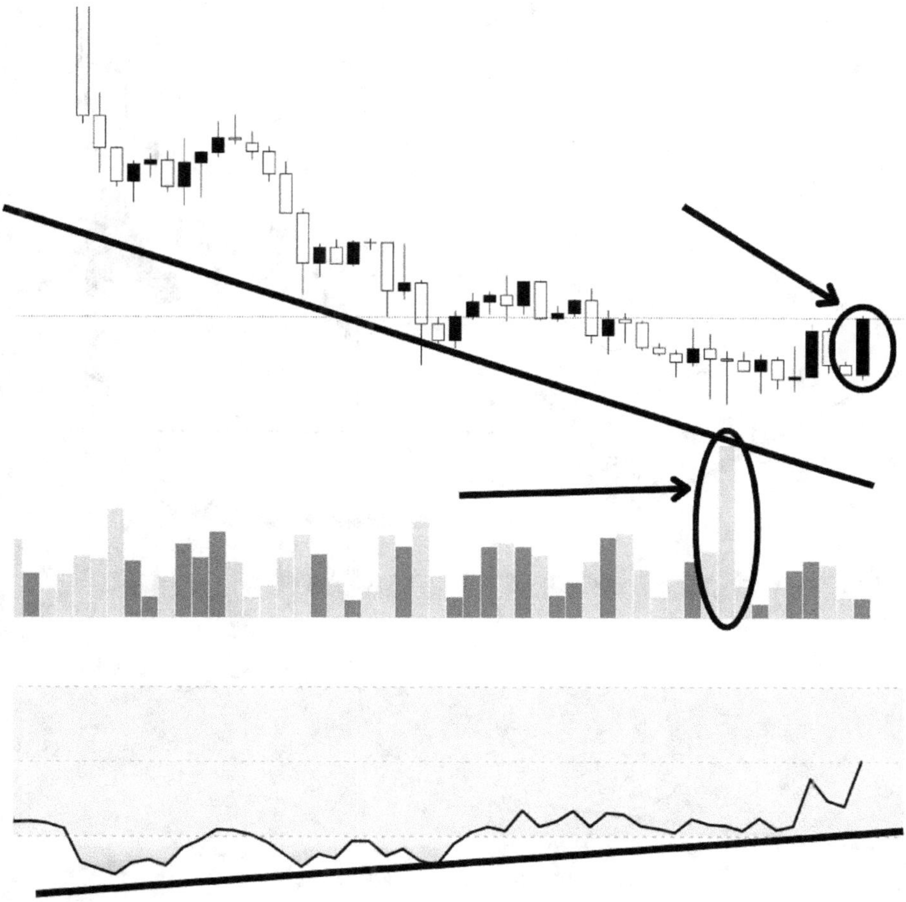

A volume spike at the divergence low, along with a bullish engulfing candlestick confirm the reversal to the upside, enter a long position at the close of the bullish engulfing candlestick

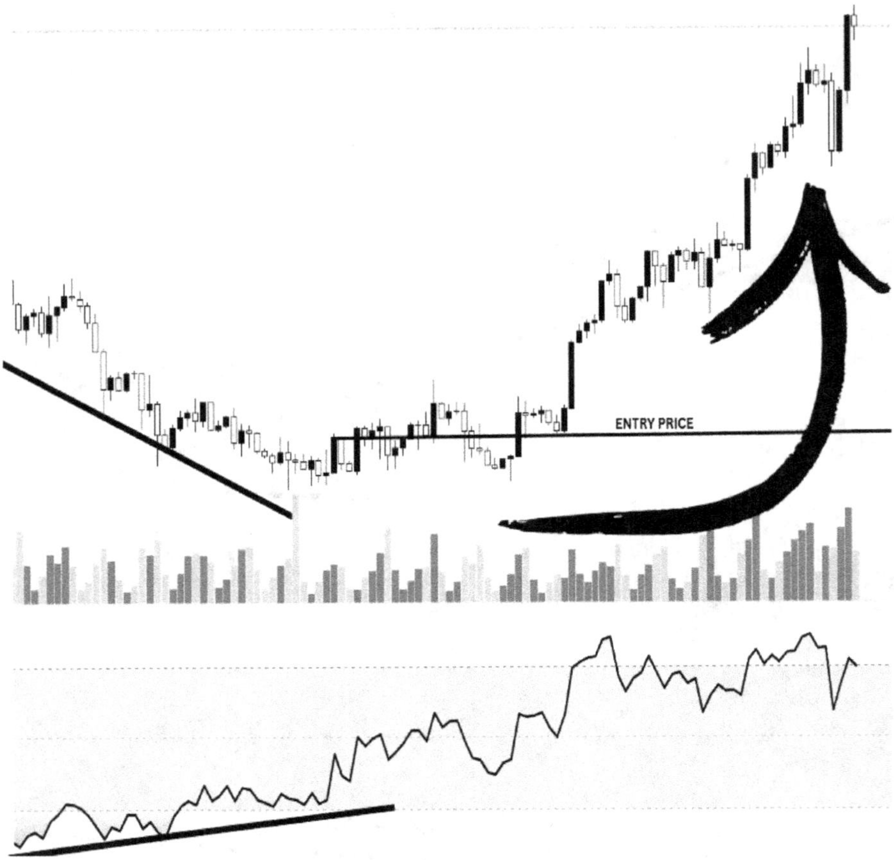

Chart shows a strong move to the upside

Example (bearish):

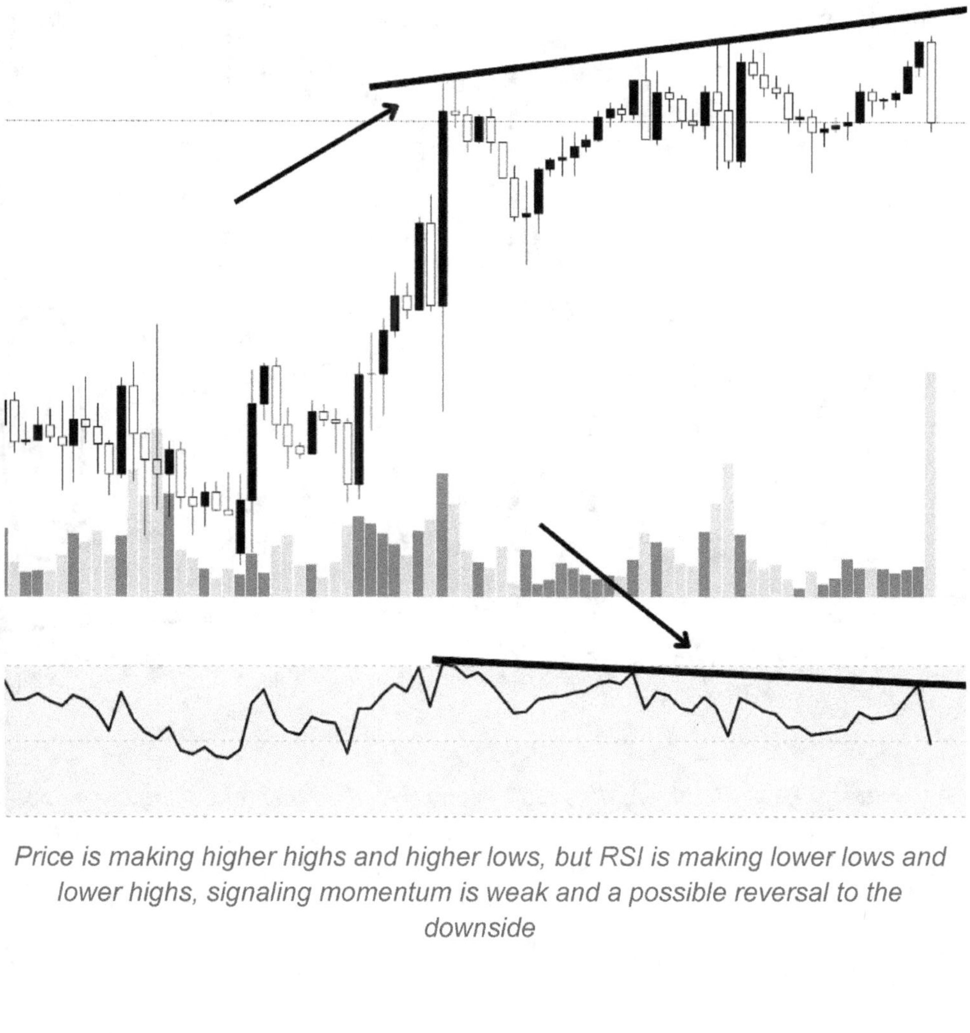

Price is making higher highs and higher lows, but RSI is making lower lows and lower highs, signaling momentum is weak and a possible reversal to the downside

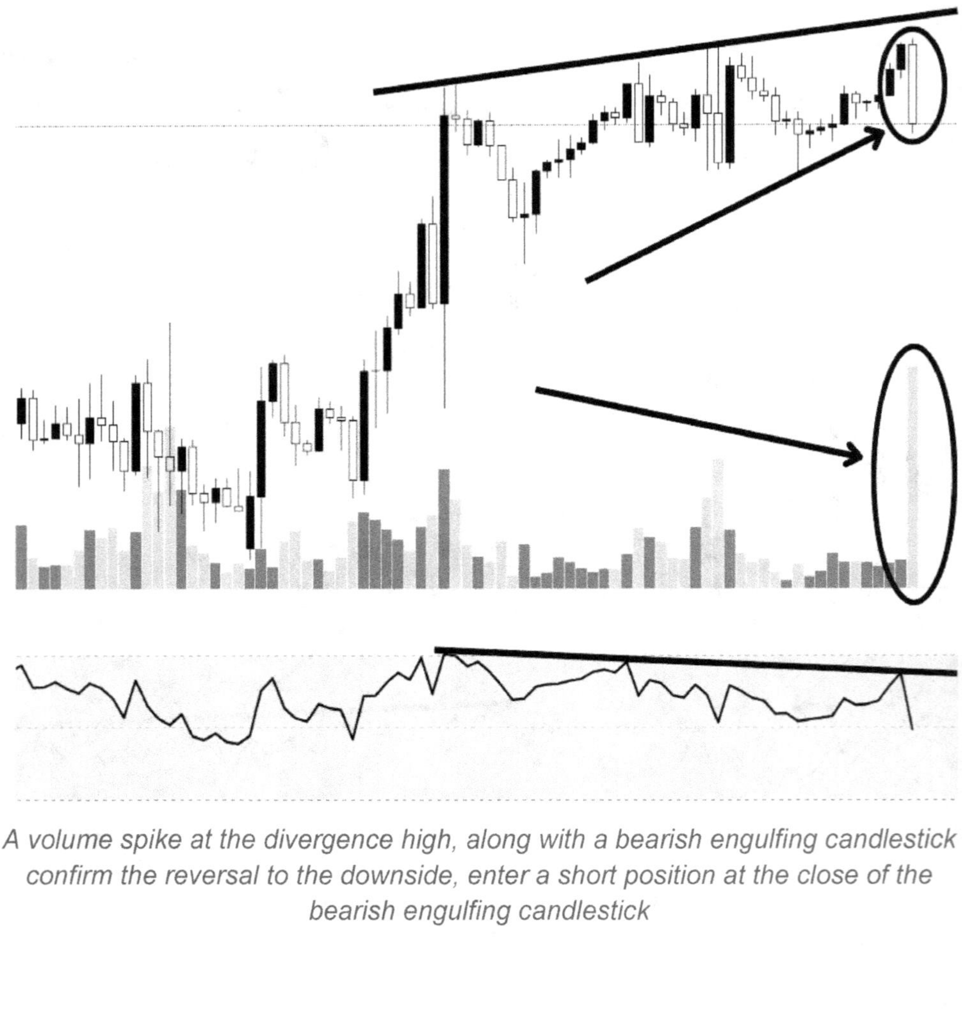

A volume spike at the divergence high, along with a bearish engulfing candlestick confirm the reversal to the downside, enter a short position at the close of the bearish engulfing candlestick

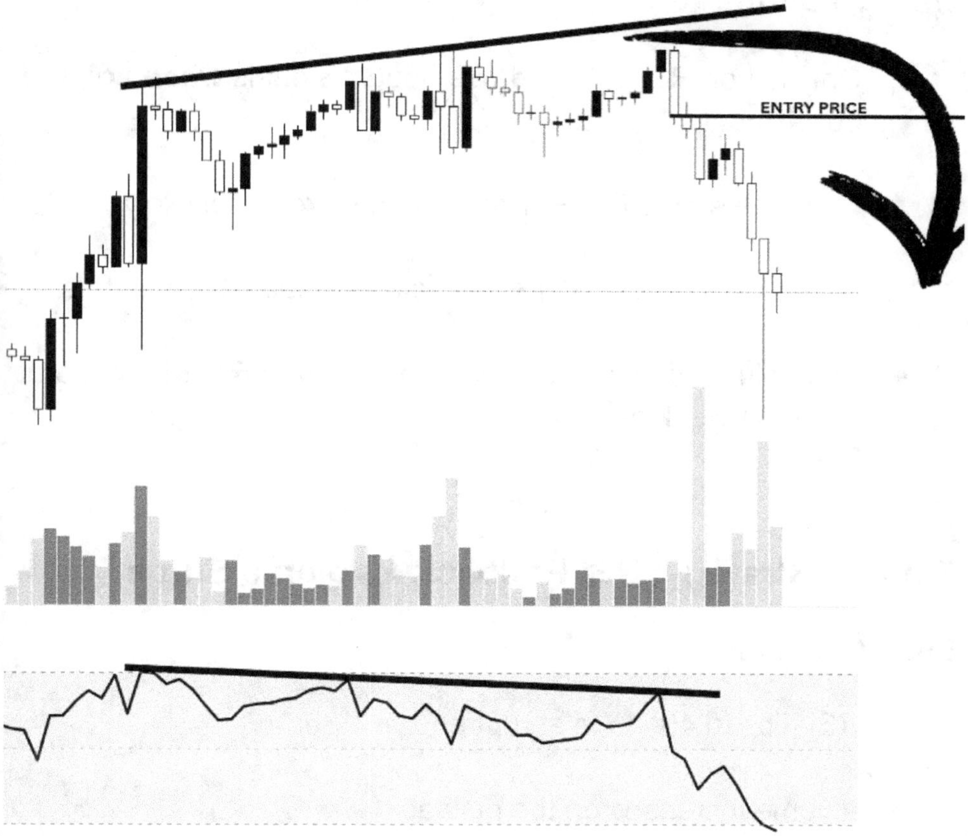

Chart shows a strong move to the downside

Using Volume to Filter RSI Signals

- Only act on RSI oversold/overbought signals **when volume confirms**:
    - Oversold RSI + rising volume = reversal likely
    - Overbought RSI + low volume = false breakout risk
- Add volume filters to eliminate **low-quality RSI signals** that occur on weak moves

Trading Strategy: RSI Pullback + Volume Surge

Entry Conditions:

- RSI dips to 40–45 in an uptrend
- Volume increases on the pullback
- Bullish engulfing or hammer candle forms on strong volume

Exit Conditions:

- RSI pushes above 70
- Volume begins to decline
- Bearish divergence appears on lower timeframe

Works well with:

- **Gold:** on retracements after news events
- **Oil:** after inventory shocks
- **Index Futures:** during midday consolidations

Summary

RSI gives you the "what," but **volume tells you the "how strong."** By combining RSI with volume, you unlock an edge that reveals the **intentions of institutional traders** and the strength (or weakness) hiding behind price action. In volatile futures markets like oil, gold, and indices, this combination can help you confirm breakouts, avoid traps, and trade with greater confidence.

Key Takeaways

➤ RSI tells you about momentum; volume confirms the strength behind it

➤ Strong RSI signals backed by high volume are more trustworthy

➤ Flat RSI + rising volume can signal traps or smart money activity

➤ RSI divergence paired with volume spikes signals high-probability reversals

➤ Filter RSI trades using volume to increase win rate and avoid fakeouts

Chapter 12

RSI + Moving Averages – Building a Complete Strategy

Introduction

When combined, the **Relative Strength Index (RSI)** and **moving averages** form a powerful trading system that captures momentum, filters out noise, and aligns entries with the overall trend. RSI provides insights into **momentum and overbought/oversold conditions**, while moving averages define **trend direction and dynamic support/resistance**. Together, they help traders avoid false signals and focus on **high-probability setups**.

Why Combine RSI and Moving Averages?

- Moving averages help determine **the trend direction** and smooth out price action
- RSI detects **momentum shifts and exhaustion points**
- Combining both helps traders:
    - Avoid trading **against the trend**
    - Confirm entries only when **momentum and trend align**
    - Exit before a **trend reversal** develops

Trend Confirmation with Moving Averages

- Use a longer-period moving average (e.g., 50 EMA or 200 SMA) to **define the trend**
- Price above the MA = **bullish bias**
- Price below the MA = **bearish bias**
- This trend filter prevents taking RSI signals that **go against the broader move**

Example (bullish):

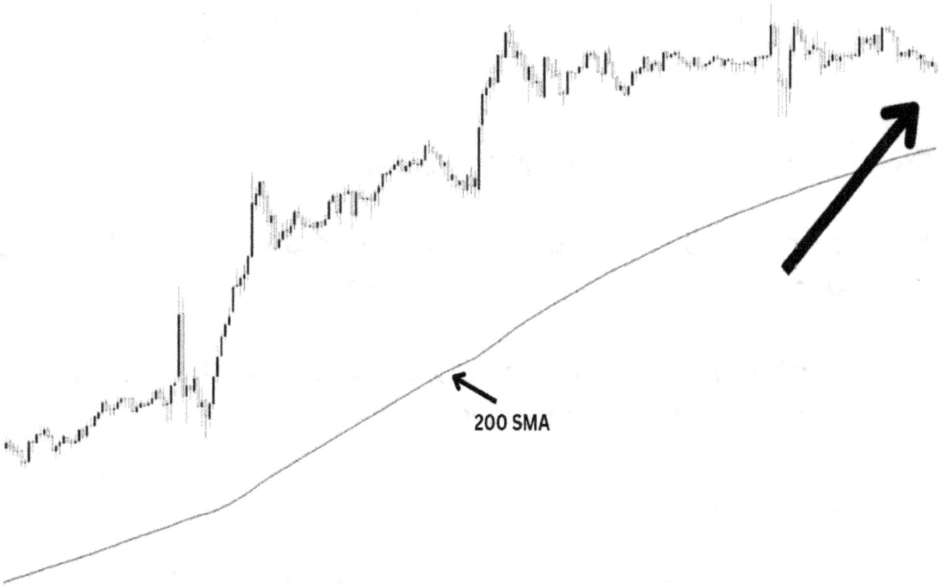

Price is trending above the 200 SMA, signaling bullish bias

Example (bearish):

Price is trending below the 200 SMA, signaling bearish bias

Entry Signals: RSI and MA Synergy

- Wait for RSI to **pull back into oversold (in uptrend)** or **overbought (in downtrend)** zones
- Look for **price action to stay above/below the moving average** during that RSI signal
- Enter when:
    - RSI reverses from oversold and price holds above the moving average (bullish)
    - RSI turns down from overbought and price holds below the moving average (bearish)

Example (bullish):

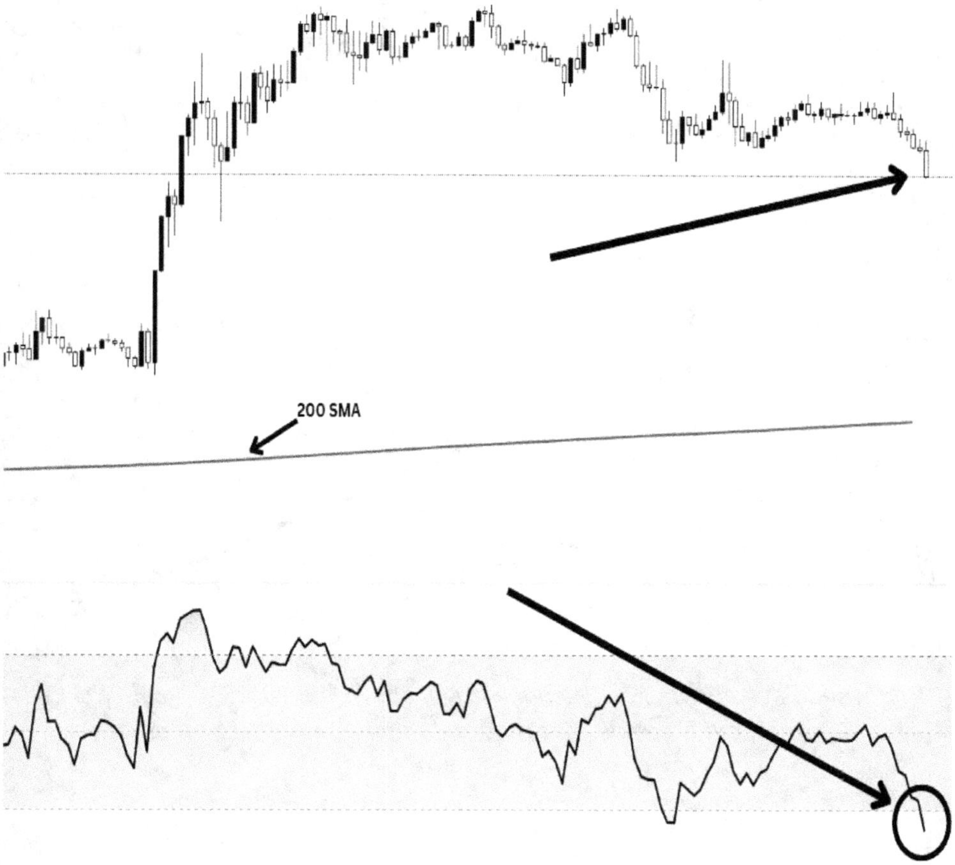

RSI falls below 30 while price is staying above the 200 SMA, signaling a potential move to the upside

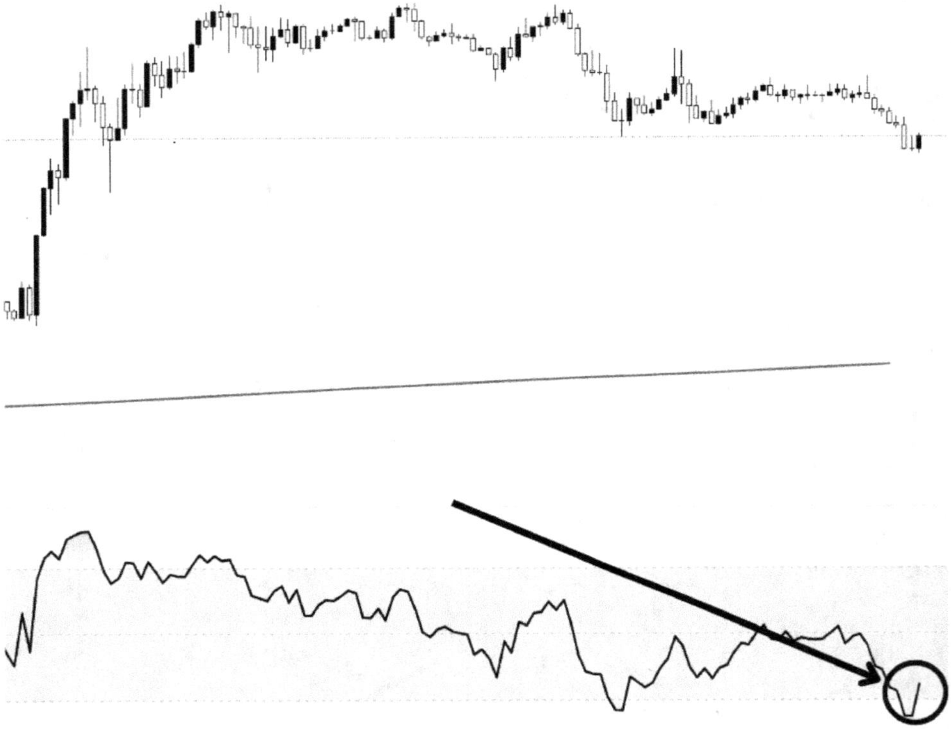

RSI crosses back above 30 while price is still above the 200 SMA, confirming the move to the upside. Enter as soon as RSI closes above 30

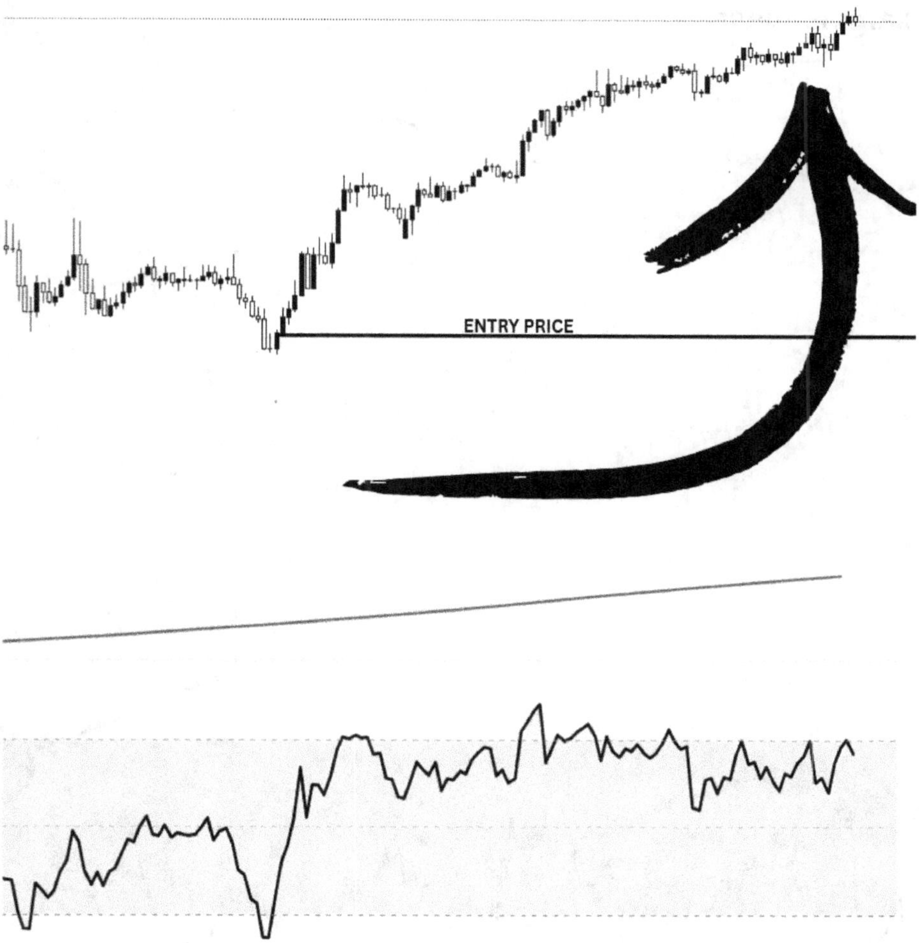

Chart shows a strong move to the upside

Example (bearish):

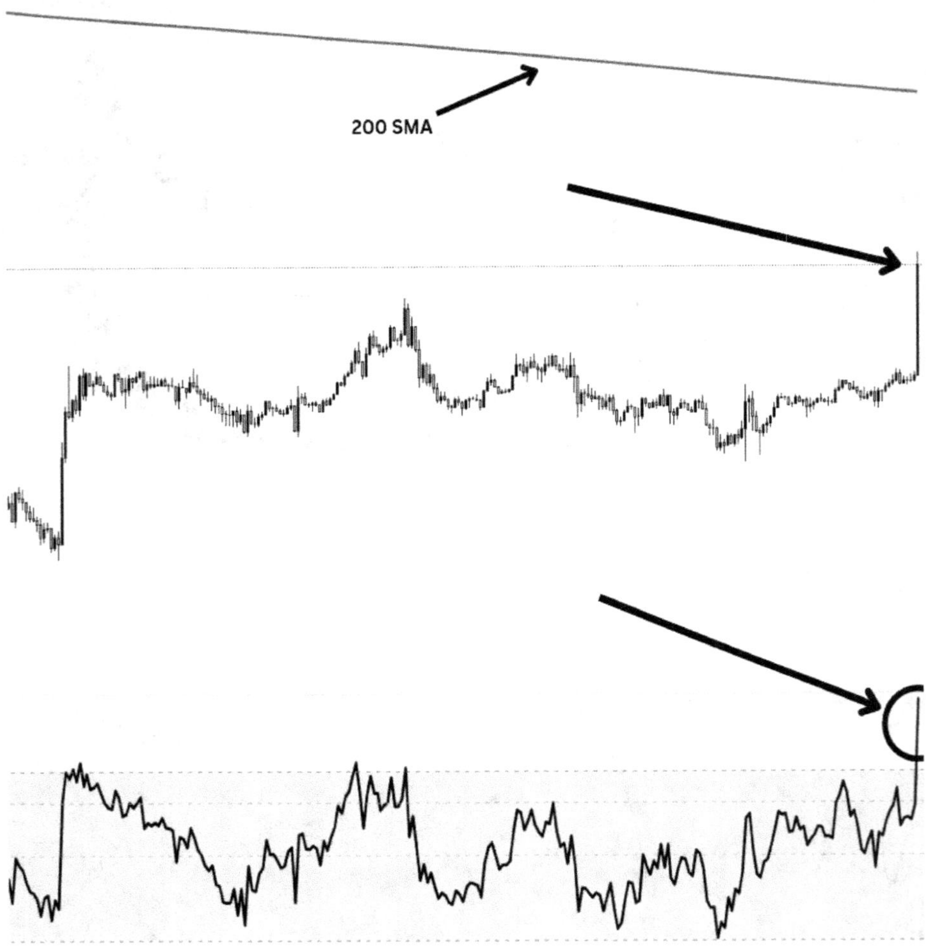

RSI crosses above 70 while price is staying below the 200 SMA, signaling a potential move to the downside

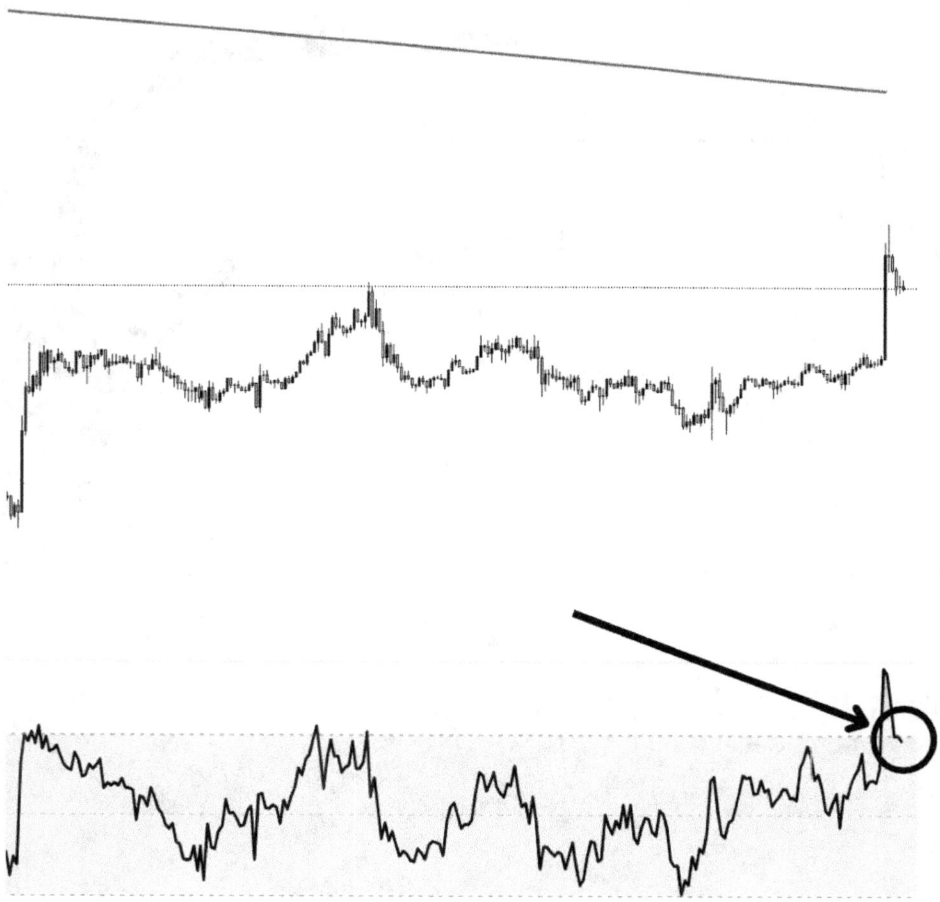

RSI falls back below 70 while price is still below the 200 SMA, confirming the move to the downside. Enter as soon as RSI closes below 70

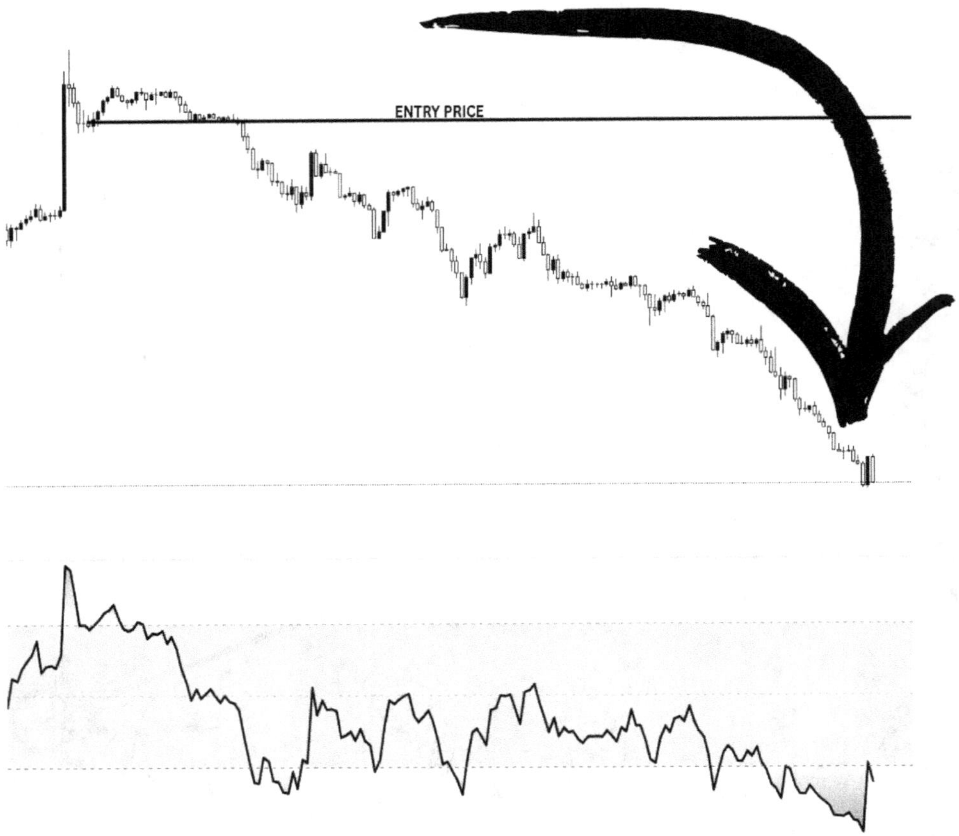

Chart shows a strong move to the downside

Using a Trailing Stop with a Moving Average After RSI Entries

Why Combine RSI with a Trailing MA Stop?

- RSI provides the **timing** of your entry—e.g., buying during a bullish RSI divergence or selling at overbought conditions.
- Moving averages act as **dynamic support/resistance** and can trail price efficiently as trends develop.
- Combining the two gives you the **best of both worlds**: a precise entry with a trend-respecting exit.

How to Set It Up

Step 1: Apply a Moving Average

- Use a short- to mid-term MA such as the **9 EMA**, **20 EMA**, or **21 SMA** to trail your stop.
- This MA will now become your **dynamic exit guide** along with confirming entries.

Step 2: Enter Using RSI + MA Rules

- For example, enter long when RSI crosses below and back above 30 and stays above MA.

Step 3: Place Your Trailing Stop

- As the trade progresses in your favor, move your stop loss **just below the moving average** (for long trades) or above it (for short trades).

- You can use either:

    - A **fixed buffer** (e.g., 1% below the MA), or

    - A **price action buffer**, such as the most recent swing low.

Step 4: Exit When Price Closes Beyond the Moving Average

- If price closes decisively below your chosen moving average, **exit the trade** to protect your gains.

- Optionally, wait for two closes below to reduce the chance of being shaken out by noise.

Example (bullish):

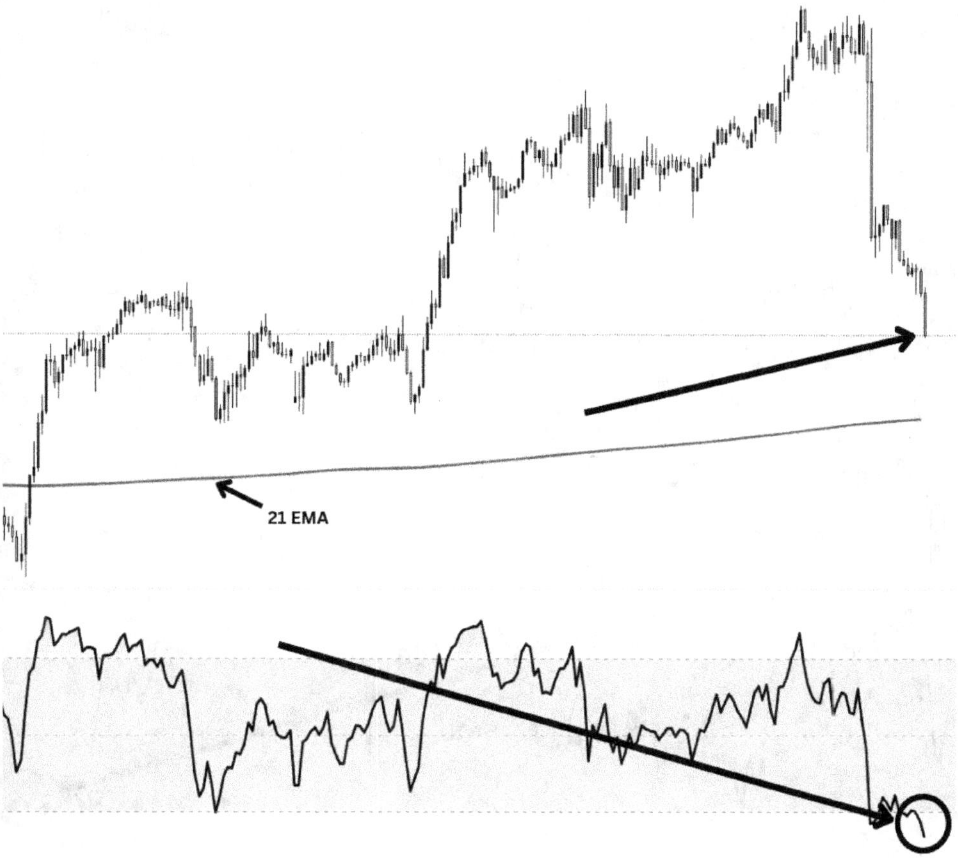

RSI falls below 30 while price is staying above the 21 EMA, signaling a potential move to the upside

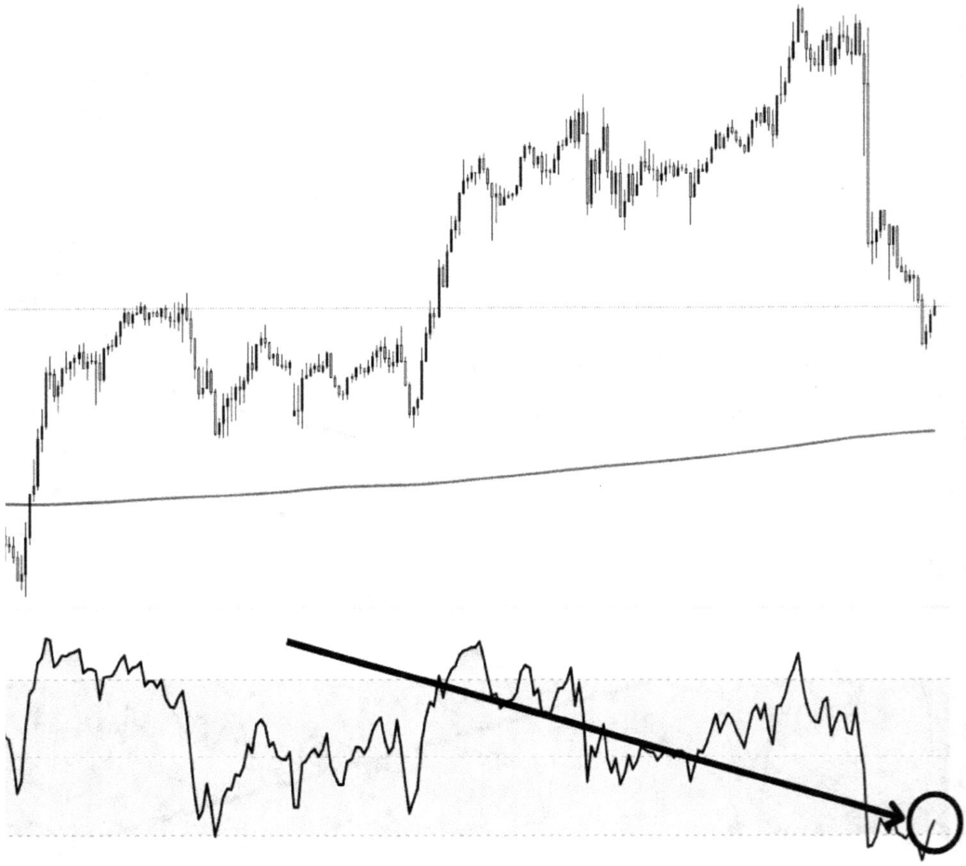

RSI crosses back above 30 while price is still above the 21 EMA, confirming the move to the upside. Enter as soon as RSI closes above 30

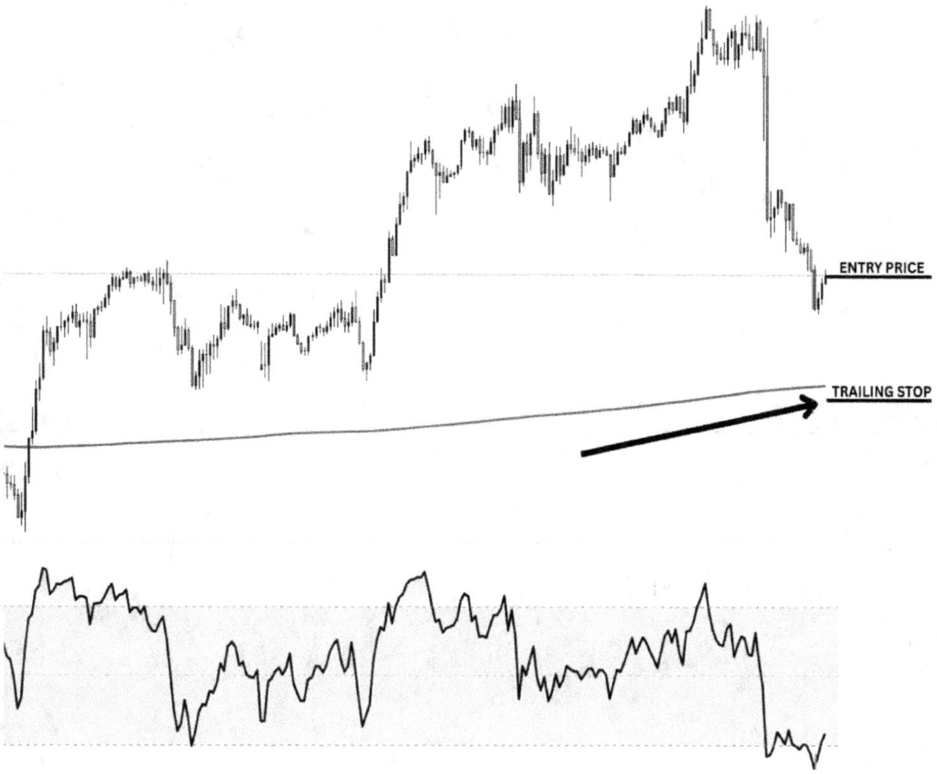

Place a trailing stop to just below the 21 EMA, as the trade progresses to the upside, continuously move the stop to just below the 21 EMA

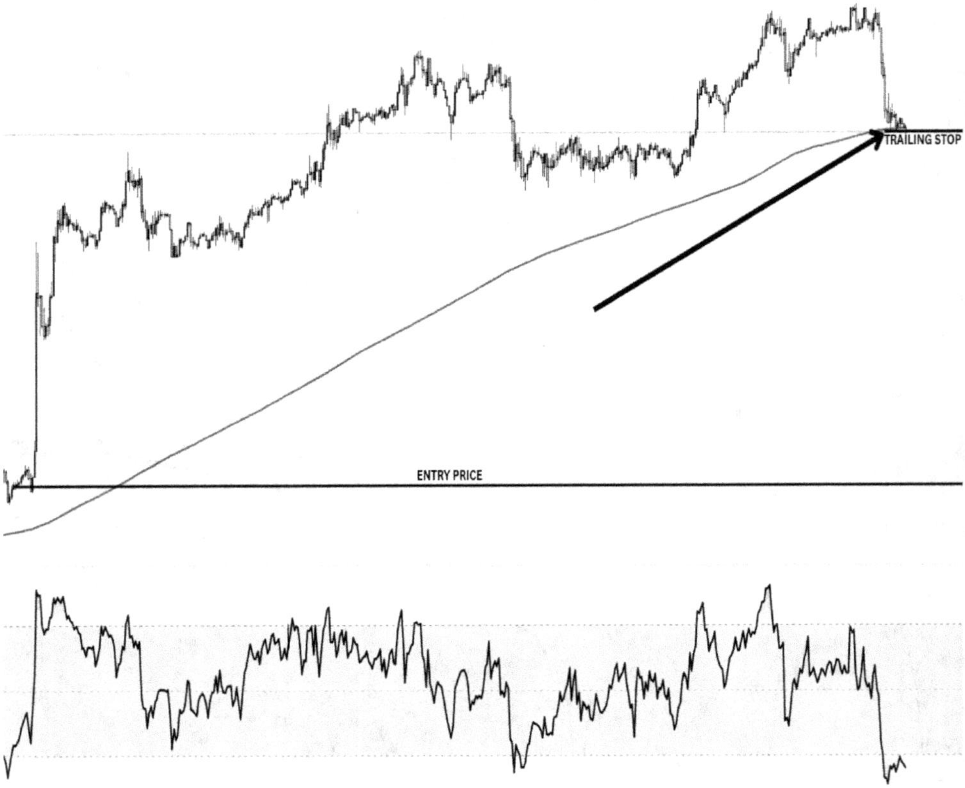

Chart shows a strong move to the upside while price falls below the 21 EMA, which hits the trailing stop and exits the position

Example (bearish):

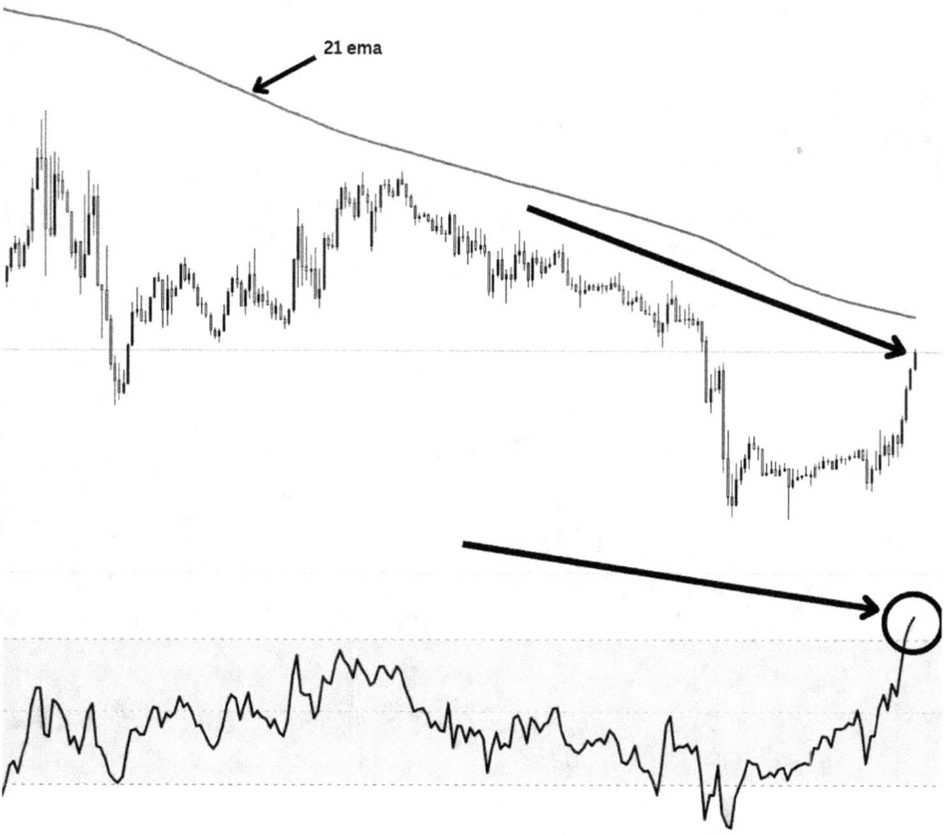

RSI crosses above 70 while price is staying below the 21 EMA, signaling a potential move to the downside

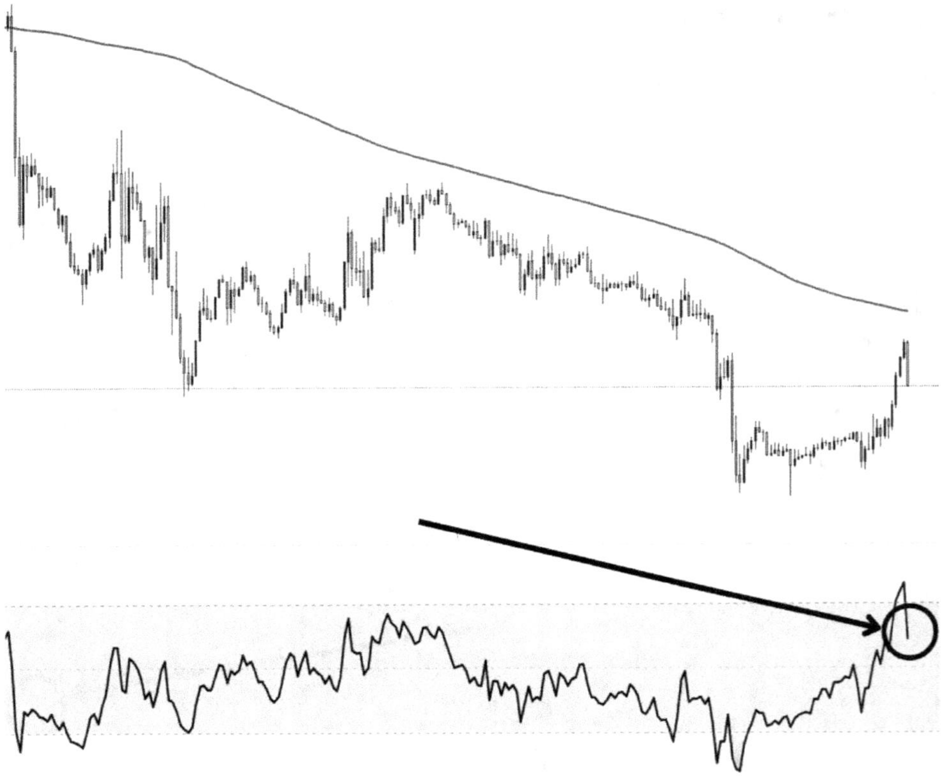

RSI crosses back below 70 while price is still below the 21 EMA, confirming the move to the downside. Enter as soon as RSI closes below 70

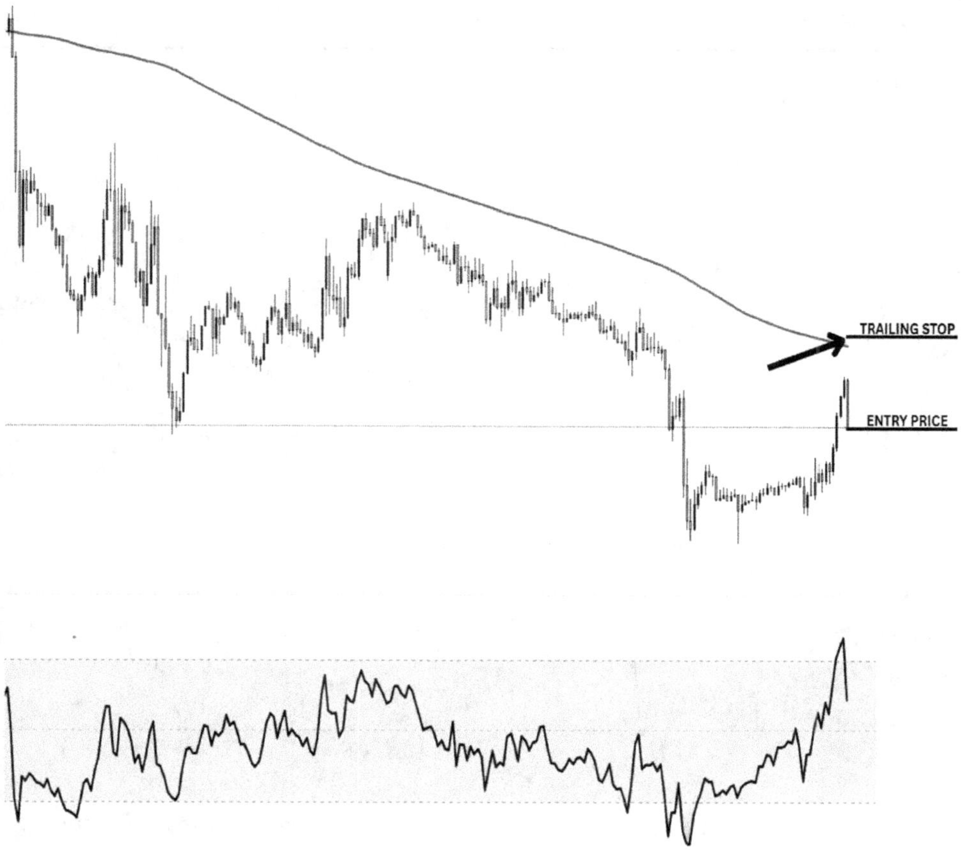

Place a trailing stop to just above the 21 EMA, as the trade progresses to the downside, continuously move the stop to just above the 21 EMA

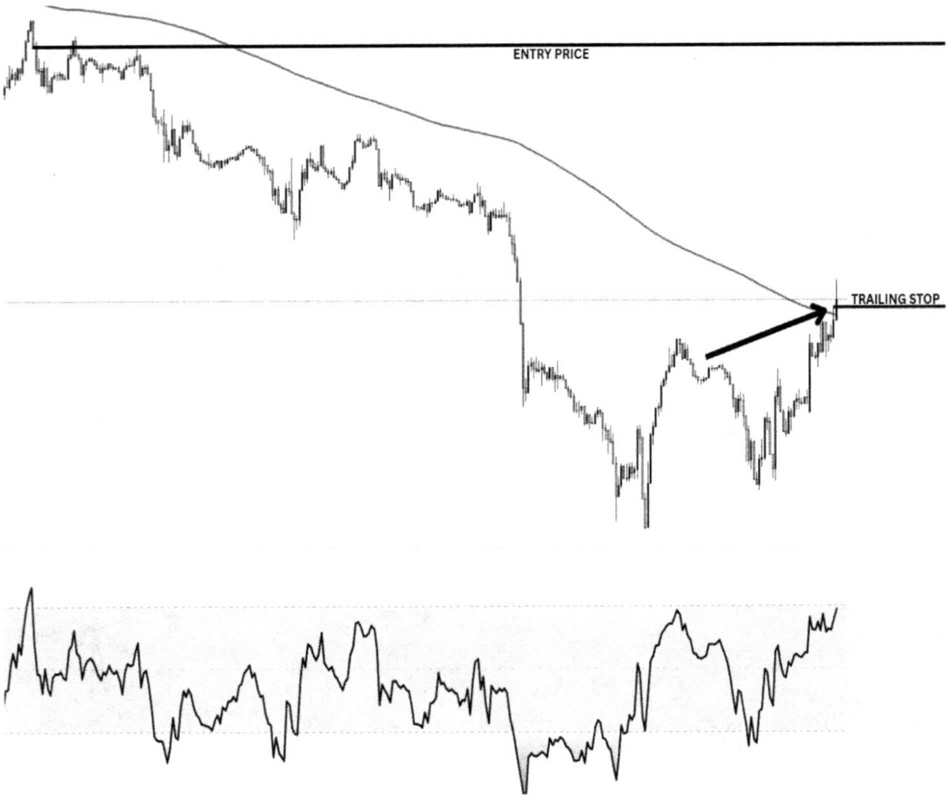

Chart shows a strong move to the downside while price crosses above the 21 EMA, which hits the trailing stop and exits the position

Filtering Whipsaws with Trend Alignment

- RSI alone can give **false reversal signals** in strong trends
- Use MA to **filter out bad RSI trades**:
    - Ignore RSI overbought in a strong uptrend (stay long-biased)
    - Ignore RSI oversold in a strong downtrend (stay short-biased)
- This keeps you **on the right side of momentum**

Using RSI for Timing, MA for Direction

- Moving average = **trend bias**
- RSI = **entry timing**
- This combo allows:
    - Precision entries after pullbacks
    - Confident trend continuation trades
    - Avoidance of early reversals

Tips for Success with This Strategy

- Avoid **choppy markets** where price flips above/below MA repeatedly
- Use a **higher timeframe moving average** to validate trend (i.e., 4H 50 EMA)
- Combine with **candlestick confirmation** near MA + RSI level
- Avoid entries when RSI and price **diverge significantly** (signals weakening move)

Summary

Pairing RSI with moving averages creates a **trend-following system** that's flexible, reliable, and adaptable across asset classes. RSI tells you **when** momentum is shifting, while moving averages tell you **where** price is likely to react. When you combine both tools with a disciplined approach, you can filter out noise, align with the dominant trend, and confidently time your trades in oil, gold, or index futures.

Key Takeaways

➤ Moving averages define the trend, while RSI identifies momentum shifts and entry timing

➤ Only take RSI signals that align with the moving average trend to avoid false setups

➤ Use MA as dynamic support/resistance and RSI as the trigger for entry

➤ Use this combo across oil, gold, and index futures with slight adjustments to timeframe and RSI periods

➤ Exit when RSI loses momentum or price breaks the moving average trend structure

Chapter 13

Custom RSI Zones – Breaking Free of 70/30

Introduction

Most traders rely on the standard RSI thresholds of **70 for overbought** and **30 for oversold**. But markets aren't always that simple. In different volatility environments and market structures, those static numbers can lead to **missed trades, early exits, or late entries**. In this chapter, we'll break free of the traditional RSI boundaries and explore how **custom RSI zones** can provide more precise and adaptive signals—especially in oil, gold, and index futures.

Why the Standard 70/30 Doesn't Always Work

- Markets trend more often than they range—yet 70/30 was built for **range-bound behavior**.
- In strong bull markets, RSI may **stay above 50** and rarely touch 30.
- In strong downtrends, RSI can remain **below 50**, never reaching 70.
- Rigid RSI settings can lead to **overcautious or mistimed trades** in real-time conditions.

The Power of Custom RSI Zones

- Custom zones adapt RSI to the **current market regime**—trending or ranging.
- This allows for **earlier entries**, **stronger trend-following**, and **more intelligent reversals**.
- Institutions often use **dynamic RSI filters**—you can too.

Custom Zones for Bullish Trending Markets

- Instead of waiting for RSI to drop to 30, consider **40 or even 50** as "oversold" in a strong uptrend.
- RSI rarely drops below 40 when bulls are in control.
- In uptrends:
    - RSI **pullbacks to 40–50 = buy zone**
    - RSI breaking above 60–70 = **momentum continuation**
- Look for **bullish candles or support bounces** when RSI dips into the custom bullish zone.

Example (Oil Futures):

- During oil rallies, RSI may bounce repeatedly off 45.
- Using 45 instead of 30 avoids missing excellent buy-the-dip setups.

Custom Zones for Bearish Trending Markets

- In a downtrend, RSI often **resists crossing above 60**.
- Overbought conditions can occur at **55 or even 50** in strong bearish markets.
- In downtrends:
    - RSI rallies to 50–60 = **short zone**
    - RSI breaking below 40–30 = **trend acceleration**
- Look for **bearish engulfing candles or resistance reactions** in this custom zone.

Example (S&P 500 Futures):

- During sharp corrections, RSI may fail near 55 several times.
- Using 55 instead of 70 gets you in earlier and avoids the lag of waiting for textbook overbought.

Custom RSI Zones in Range-Bound Markets

- Ranges are where **traditional RSI shines**, but can still be optimized.
- In tighter ranges, you might use:
  - **65 for overbought**, **35 for oversold**
  - Or even **60/40** for choppy sideways action.
- This tightens your signals and gives more **frequent trade opportunities** without overreaching.

Example (Gold Futures):

- When gold is consolidating, RSI may reverse repeatedly at 60 and 40.
- Adapting to these tighter zones lets you catch **mean-reversion setups faster**.

How to Define the Right Custom RSI Zones

- **Step 1: Identify Market Context**
  Is the market trending or ranging? Trending = shift RSI zones. Ranging = standard zones work fine.
- **Step 2: Analyze RSI Behavior**
  Look at the past 20–50 bars and see where RSI has respected levels.
  Has it been bouncing off 42? Failing at 58? Use those as

your new thresholds.

- **Step 3: Combine with Price Action or MAs**
  Use candlestick setups or moving averages to **confirm RSI reactions** in your custom zones.

Adjusting Zones Based on Volatility

- In **high-volatility environments**, RSI tends to move more aggressively—widen zones slightly.
- In **low-volatility conditions**, RSI may react more subtly—tighten your zones.
- You can even **blend with ATR** (Average True Range) to fine-tune zone responsiveness.

Backtesting Your Custom RSI Zones

- Use charting tools like **TradingView** or **ThinkorSwim** to replay market conditions.
- Backtest your custom zones on:
  - Crude oil (CL)
  - Gold (GC)
  - S&P 500 (ES)

- Measure how well your adjusted levels capture:
    - **Pullbacks**
    - **Breakouts**
    - **Divergences**

Tips for Success

- Treat custom RSI zones as **flexible, not fixed**—adjust as market structure evolves.
- Keep track of your most effective custom levels in a journal.
- Use custom RSI zones **in conjunction with candlesticks, trendlines, and MAs**—never isolate them.

Summary

The default 70/30 RSI settings are useful—but they're not optimal in all market conditions. By creating **custom RSI zones** based on trend strength, volatility, and asset behavior, you unlock **greater timing precision, earlier entries**, and **cleaner trend participation**. Whether you're trading oil, gold, or index futures, understanding how to flex RSI zones will make your edge sharper and more consistent.

Key Takeaways

➤ Standard RSI zones (70/30) are often too rigid for real-world trading conditions.

➤ In strong uptrends, use **40–50 RSI** as the new "buy zone."

➤ In downtrends, treat **50–60 RSI** as potential reversal zones for shorts.

➤ In tight ranges, adjust RSI thresholds to **60/40 or 65/35** for faster signals.

➤ Backtest and adapt your custom RSI zones regularly to match changing volatility and price structure.

Chapter 14

RSI Automation – Coding RSI Into Your Trading Systems

Introduction

The Relative Strength Index (RSI) is a powerful tool for gauging momentum and timing trades. But to truly unlock its potential—especially in fast-paced markets like oil, gold, and index futures—you need to remove emotion and delay from execution. That's where automation comes in.

Coding RSI into your trading systems allows for **real-time execution**, **precise backtesting**, and **emotionless discipline**. Whether you're using Pine Script in TradingView, Python, or even no-code platforms, this chapter shows how to turn RSI into a rules-based system that can run 24/7.

Benefits of Automating RSI Strategies

- Eliminates emotional trading mistakes
- Increases consistency and reliability
- Enables high-speed execution, especially for short-term trades
- Allows for backtesting and strategy optimization
- Lets traders scale to more markets without manual overload

Step 1: Define Your RSI-Based Rules

Before coding, you need clear rules based on RSI logic:

- **Buy Signals**
    - RSI crosses above 30 (oversold recovery)
    - RSI crosses above 50 (bullish momentum confirmation)
- **Sell Signals**
    - RSI crosses below 70 (overbought fade)
    - RSI crosses below 50 (bearish momentum shift)
- **Optional Filters**
    - Trend filter with a moving average
    - Time of day or session filter
    - Volume spike confirmation

Step 2: Choose a Platform for Automation

Here are the best options depending on your skill level and goals:

1. TradingView (Pine Script):

- Great for visual RSI strategies with chart overlays
- Allows automation via webhook alerts
- Integrates easily with third-party automation tools (e.g., 3Commas, Zapier)

2. MetaTrader 4/5 (MQL4/MQL5):

- Ideal for algorithmic RSI trading in forex and futures
- Allows complete strategy automation including entry, stop-loss, and take-profit
- Requires programming knowledge

3. Python (with libraries like Backtrader or QuantConnect):

- Best for custom RSI logic, large-scale backtesting, and advanced automation
- Supports data feeds for futures (through broker APIs like Interactive Brokers)

4. No-Code Tools (e.g., Capitalise.ai, Trade Ideas):

- Perfect for traders with no coding experience
- Use natural language like:
    - "Buy ES futures when RSI(14) crosses above 30 and price above 9 EMA"
- Limited to supported brokers and basic logic

Step 3: Code an Example RSI Strategy (Pine Script – TradingView)

Example script:

```
//@version=5

strategy("RSI Breakout Strategy", overlay=true)

rsiSource = close

rsiPeriod = 14

rsiValue = ta.rsi(rsiSource, rsiPeriod)


// Entry rules

longCondition = ta.crossover(rsiValue, 30)

shortCondition = ta.crossunder(rsiValue, 70)


// Execution

if (longCondition)

    strategy.entry("Long", strategy.long)


if (shortCondition)

    strategy.entry("Short", strategy.short)
```

- This script enters long when RSI crosses above 30
- Enters short when RSI crosses below 70
- Add stop-loss, take-profit, or MA filters as needed

Step 4: Backtest and Optimize

- Use **TradingView's strategy tester** or **Backtrader in Python**
- Analyze metrics:
    - Win rate
    - Profit factor
    - Max drawdown
    - Sharpe ratio
- Test across different futures:
    - Oil (CL): Trend-based RSI system
    - Gold (GC): Range-to-trend hybrid RSI logic
    - Index Futures (ES/NQ): Fast 9-period RSI + volume spike combo

Step 5: Paper Trade or Simulate First

- Always test in a **simulated environment**
- Confirm trade execution timing, slippage, and performance
- Use platforms like:
    - **TradingView + paper broker sim**
    - **MetaTrader demo accounts**
    - **IBKR Paper Trading** for real futures simulation

Step 6: Deploy Live with Risk Management

- Use tight automation guardrails:
    - Max daily loss limit
    - Max position size
    - Real-time trade logs
- Monitor trades even if automated
- RSI strategies can **underperform in choppy conditions**, so include a kill switch or pause logic

Summary

Automating RSI strategies puts your trading on autopilot without sacrificing control or precision. With the right rules, platform, and risk controls, RSI automation gives you a consistent, disciplined edge in volatile futures markets. Whether you're scalping oil, swinging gold, or trend-riding the S&P 500, automated RSI execution can improve speed, reduce emotion, and unlock scalable consistency.

Key Takeaways

➤ RSI can be automated for fast, emotionless execution using tools like TradingView, Python, or no-code platforms

➤ Define your RSI signals clearly (crosses, divergences, filters) before building the system

➤ TradingView's Pine Script is excellent for visual RSI systems and real-time alerts

➤ Always backtest RSI logic and optimize settings for each market before going live

➤ Paper trade to ensure reliability, then use risk management when deploying live in futures markets

Chapter 15

RSI Psychology – Why It Works and Why It Fails

Introduction

The Relative Strength Index (RSI) is one of the most widely used technical indicators in trading—and for good reason. It captures key psychological turning points in the market by measuring the velocity of price movements. But like any indicator, RSI is not flawless. It's important to understand the psychological principles that make it effective—and the psychological traps that can cause it to fail.

This chapter explores **why RSI works**, the **behavioral forces** behind its signals, and the **common trader mistakes** that lead to misinterpreting or misusing it.

The Psychology Behind RSI

- RSI tracks **momentum**—a reflection of **fear and greed cycles** in price movement
- When RSI is high (near 70+), it reflects **euphoria**, trend exhaustion, or overextension
- When RSI is low (near 30−), it reflects **panic selling**, capitulation, or exhaustion
- RSI reversal signals often appear **at emotional extremes**, when most traders are acting irrationally

Why RSI Works

- **Crowd Behavior Predictability**: When too many market participants are long or short, price tends to reverse as the trade becomes crowded

- **Mean Reversion Tendencies**: Markets often "snap back" to their mean after a strong move—RSI identifies these overextended zones

- **Self-Fulfilling Signal**: Since many traders watch RSI, especially 70/30 levels, it often creates reactions around these zones

- **Stops and Liquidation Events**: Oversold RSI often means forced selling; oversold conditions dry up, leading to bounce opportunities

When RSI is Most Reliable

- **Clear Trending Conditions with Momentum Breaks**: RSI divergences are strong signals during fading momentum in trends

- **Overbought/Oversold Extremes with Confirmation**: RSI works well when paired with candlestick signals or volume spikes

- **Range-Bound Markets**: RSI excels at timing reversals between known horizontal support and resistance zones

- **After Economic News Shocks**: Post-news volatility often creates emotional RSI spikes, then mean-reverts quickly

Why RSI Fails

- **Traders Assume Overbought Means Reversal**: RSI can stay overbought or oversold for extended periods during strong trends

- **Using RSI in Isolation**: Relying on RSI without confirmation (like price action, trend direction, or volume) increases false signals

- **Ignoring Market Context**: RSI works differently in trending vs. choppy markets. Traders applying it the same way everywhere get burned

- **Overreacting to Crossovers**: RSI crossing 70/30 doesn't guarantee reversal—it might just be momentum continuation

Emotional Traps Traders Fall Into

- **Premature Entries**: Traders jump into trades just because RSI hits a level, ignoring broader structure
- **Confirmation Bias**: Traders see what they want when RSI supports their opinion, even if the setup is weak
- **Fear of Missing Out**: RSI nearing extremes makes traders anxious—they act impulsively instead of waiting for signals
- **Revenge Trading**: After an RSI trade fails, traders double down irrationally, blaming the market rather than poor execution

Psychological Tips to Use RSI More Effectively

- **Zoom Out First**: Check the higher timeframe trend before acting on lower timeframe RSI signals
- **Pair RSI with Structure**: Look for RSI signals at key support/resistance, trendlines, or Fibonacci zones
- **Wait for Confirmation**: Use RSI divergence, candle patterns, or volume shifts to confirm an RSI entry
- **Use RSI as a Warning, Not a Trigger**: RSI should alert you to potential setups—not be the sole reason for taking a trade
- **Avoid Random Timeframes**: Traders often apply RSI without knowing how responsive or laggy it is at that setting

Market-Specific Psychology Examples

- **Crude Oil**: During strong geopolitical trends, RSI can stay overbought for days. Wait for volume or reversal candles before trusting a reversal.
- **Gold**: Gold traders overreact to inflation and fear-based headlines—RSI extremes during news can fade fast.
- **Index Futures (ES/NQ)**: Algorithmic buying pushes RSI into persistent zones. Trust breakouts more than reversals unless you see exhaustion.

Summary

RSI works because it reflects human behavior in the market—emotional overextensions followed by corrections. However, its simplicity can deceive traders who don't consider market context or confirmation. Understanding **why RSI works** and **when it fails** can turn this basic tool into a psychological weapon in your trading arsenal. When used with discipline, RSI can help you anticipate crowd emotion, avoid traps, and time your trades with greater confidence.

Key Takeaways

➤ RSI is powerful because it reflects crowd psychology and emotional extremes

➤ It works best in range-bound markets, with confirmations like candlestick patterns or volume shifts

➤ RSI often fails when traders use it in isolation or against the dominant trend

➤ Avoid emotional mistakes like FOMO, premature entries, and revenge trades

➤ Always consider trend context and confluence when using RSI for decision-making

Chapter 16

The Complete RSI Blueprint – Rules, Filters & Optimization

Introduction

To trade RSI like a pro, you need more than just recognizing overbought and oversold levels—you need a complete system. A true RSI blueprint includes **precise rules**, **contextual filters**, and **ongoing optimization**. This chapter delivers an actionable framework to structure your RSI-based strategy with clarity and consistency.

Whether you're a swing trader, day trader, or scalper, applying this blueprint will help you reduce false signals, increase confidence, and trade the RSI like an institutional-level tool.

Core RSI Trading Rules

Start by building a solid foundation with clear RSI trading rules that govern your entries and exits.

- **Define Your Signal Type**
    - RSI cross below 30 = watch for long setup
    - RSI cross above 70 = watch for short setup
    - RSI divergence = potential reversal signal
    - RSI trendline break = possible shift in momentum
- **Entry Confirmation Rules**
    - Combine RSI signals with price action (e.g., engulfing candle, pin bar, inside bar)
    - Use confluence with support/resistance or moving averages

- Only trade signals in the direction of the higher timeframe trend

- **Exit Strategy**
    - Target 2:1 or 3:1 risk-to-reward setups
    - Exit when RSI returns to midline (50) or approaches opposite extreme
    - Use trailing stops if price gains momentum post-entry

- **Stop Loss Placement**
    - Just beyond recent swing high/low
    - Use trailing stops with MA's
    - Never place stops strictly based on RSI numbers—they don't represent price levels

Filters to Improve Accuracy

To prevent false signals and whipsaws, apply context-based filters around your RSI signals. These filters will help you isolate only the highest-probability setups.

- **Trend Filter**
    - Use moving averages (e.g., 50 EMA or 200 SMA) to determine trend bias
    - Only take RSI longs above a rising MA, or RSI shorts below a falling MA
    - Helps avoid fading strong momentum

- **Volume Confirmation**
  - Look for volume spikes or divergence with RSI for stronger conviction
  - RSI divergence + rising volume = more trustworthy reversal signal
  - Low volume = likely chop or trap
- **Time-of-Day Filter (Intraday)**
  - Avoid RSI signals during low-liquidity hours (lunchtime or overnight)
  - Focus on high-volume windows: market open, major economic releases, closing hour
- **Multi-Timeframe Filter**
  - Align lower timeframe RSI signals with higher timeframe trend direction
  - Example: Only take 5-minute RSI longs when the 1-hour RSI is above 50 and trending up
- **Candlestick Filter**
  - Combine RSI with reversal candlestick patterns like dojis, hammers, or engulfing candles
  - Prevents entering on weak, random candles

RSI Settings Optimization

Your RSI strategy is only as good as the settings behind it. Here's how to fine-tune the RSI to your market and style.

- **Default Setting (14-period RSI)**
    - Works well for swing trades and broader moves
    - May lag on fast-moving instruments like Nasdaq futures
- **Faster RSI (5–9 period)**
    - More responsive to quick moves
    - Better for scalping or aggressive intraday strategies
    - Higher chance of false signals—requires strict filters
- **Slower RSI (20–30 period)**
    - Smoother, less noise
    - Good for position traders or confirming broader trend exhaustion
    - Less signals but more reliable
- **Adjusting Overbought/Oversold Zones**
    - Aggressive approach: 80/20 for stronger moves
    - Conservative approach: 60/40 for early signals but with tighter risk
    - Customize zones based on the instrument's personality (e.g., gold often whips more than indexes)

RSI Blueprint Template (Example)

Here's a plug-and-play example of a full RSI system using the blueprint:

- **Instrument**: S&P 500 E-mini (ES)
- **Timeframe**: 5-minute chart
- **RSI Setting**: 8-period RSI
- **Entry Signal**: RSI cross below 30 + bullish engulfing candle + price at intraday support
- **Trend Filter**: Only long above 200 EMA
- **Volume Filter**: Entry only on a 2-bar volume surge
- **Stop Loss**: 1.5x ATR below candle low
- **Take Profit**: RSI back to 60 or next resistance zone
- **Session Filter**: Trade only between 9:30 AM – 11:30 AM EST

This creates a repeatable, objective framework that removes emotion from the process.

Backtesting and Optimization Tips

Once your RSI blueprint is ready, it's time to validate and improve it through testing.

- **Backtest at least 50–100 trades** using historical data
- **Track win rate, average R/R, max drawdown** to assess quality
- **Tweak one variable at a time**—settings, filters, or timeframes
- Use tools like **TradingView**, **TrendSpider**, or **Excel** for testing and journaling
- Focus on **consistency over curve fitting**—a good system performs across different market cycles

Summary

Mastering RSI isn't about guessing when a market is overbought or oversold—it's about creating a structured, rules-based framework that uses RSI intelligently in context. With clear entries, disciplined filters, optimized settings, and ongoing backtesting, you can turn RSI from a simple indicator into a high-level trading strategy. This blueprint is your foundation—refine it, personalize it, and execute it with discipline.

Key Takeaways

➤ A complete RSI blueprint includes entry rules, confirmation filters, and optimized settings

➤ RSI signals are most powerful when confirmed with price action, trend, and volume filters

➤ Custom RSI settings (like 5, 8, or 21 periods) allow you to match RSI speed to your strategy

➤ Adjusting overbought/oversold zones can improve reliability in specific markets

➤ Backtest, track performance, and refine your blueprint to achieve consistent results

Chapter 17

Mastery in Motion – Turning RSI Knowledge Into Trading Power

Conclusion

The Relative Strength Index (RSI) is more than just a line on your chart—it's a window into the emotional pulse of the market. In this book, you've learned how to interpret that pulse, use it to time your entries and exits, combine it with other tools for increased precision, and even automate it into a powerful trading system. Now, the final step is to put all that knowledge into motion—to go from *understanding* RSI to *mastering* it in real-time markets.

Reflecting on What You've Learned

Let's revisit and tie together each of the foundational pieces we've built across this journey:

Chapter 1: Understanding RSI – The Core Concepts

- Gave you the historical context and purpose of RSI—how J. Welles Wilder created it and why it's still a staple among top traders decades later. You discovered that RSI is not just a momentum indicator; it's a measure of overbought and oversold sentiment—a psychological map of traders' behavior.

Chapter 2: Understanding RSI Settings – Periods, Speeds & Sensitivity

- Helped you decode the mechanics behind RSI's movement. You learned how RSI is calculated and why the 14-period setting remains a default, yet modifiable, choice depending on strategy needs.

Chapter 3: Setting Up RSI on Popular Trading Platforms

- Ensured you were ready to put RSI theory into action by walking you through the setup process on TradingView, MetaTrader, and Thinkorswim. You learned how to adjust RSI settings, apply it to your charts, create alerts, and visualize it with clarity. Whether you're a desktop trader or using mobile tools, this chapter made sure your RSI setup is clean, efficient, and ready for execution.

Chapter 4: Mastering RSI Entry and Exit Signals – How to Trade With Precision

- Introduced you to the basic overbought and oversold thresholds that most traders begin with. These gave you a foundational framework to recognize potential reversals or trend continuations.

Chapter 5: RSI and Trend Analysis – Using RSI to Confirm Trend Strength and Direction

- Showed you how RSI behaves during trending markets. You discovered that RSI can stay "overbought" or "oversold" for extended periods during strong trends, and how adjusting your interpretation avoids premature exits.

Chapter 6: RSI Divergence Mastery – Spotting Reversals Before They Happen

- Unlocked one of the most powerful predictive tools in technical analysis—divergence. You learned to identify both regular and hidden divergence, and how each type signals potential market turning points. We explored bullish and bearish setups, how to confirm them with price action and volume, and even how to avoid false signals using structure and confluence. This chapter sharpened your edge in anticipating momentum shifts before the rest of the market catches on.

Chapter 7: RSI in Consolidation – Trading the Range with Confidence

- Taught you how to harness RSI's power in non-trending markets. Instead of waiting for breakouts, you learned how to spot high-probability setups within tight price ranges by reading RSI overbought and oversold signals in sideways zones. We covered how to avoid traps, use RSI failure swings, and time your entries and exits based on RSI reversals at range extremes. You now know how to profit in quiet markets while most traders sit on the sidelines.

Chapter 8: RSI Breakout Confirmation – Separating Fakeouts from Real Moves

- Taught you how to use RSI as a powerful confirmation tool during market breakouts. Instead of blindly chasing breakouts, you learned how to analyze RSI behavior to confirm momentum and strength—separating real moves from traps. You discovered how to spot RSI shifts above 50 during bullish breakouts, and how bearish breakouts align with RSI dropping below 50. With this knowledge, you're now equipped to filter out false signals and only enter trades backed by strong RSI momentum.

Chapter 9: RSI and Candlestick Signals – Precision Entries

- Gave you the tools to sharpen your entries by combining RSI signals with candlestick confirmation. You learned how to align RSI overbought/oversold conditions with powerful candlestick patterns—like pin bars, engulfing candles, and hammers—to catch high-probability reversals or breakouts. This chapter emphasized confluence-based trading, where you wait for RSI to signal a setup and then use candlesticks to fine-tune the exact moment to enter. By mastering this approach, you're no longer guessing—you're trading with precision and timing.

Chapter 10: RSI and Multi-Timeframe Analysis

- Introduced you to the power of stacking RSI signals across different timeframes to dramatically boost your accuracy. You learned how to confirm lower-timeframe trades with higher-timeframe RSI trends, and how to avoid trading against dominant market momentum. This chapter showed you how to align your entries with the broader context—using a top-down approach where the higher timeframe gives direction, and the lower timeframe provides timing. By using RSI this way, you now have a blueprint for filtering noise, avoiding traps, and timing trades like a pro.

Chapter 11: RSI and Volume – Uncovering Hidden Strength

- Revealed how combining RSI with volume analysis uncovers what price action alone can't always show. You learned how to spot divergences between momentum and participation, identifying moments when price may be moving on weak volume or coiling for a breakout with strong volume confirmation. This chapter emphasized that RSI without volume can mislead, but when paired properly, it becomes a far more powerful signal—helping you detect false breakouts, trend exhaustion, and breakout conviction.

Chapter 12: RSI + Moving Averages – Building a Complete Strategy

- Showed how pairing RSI with moving averages creates a structured, rules-based system that adapts to trends, reversals, and ranging environments. You learned how moving averages can filter RSI entries, define trend direction, and provide dynamic support/resistance zones for better entries and exits. This chapter also covered crossover strategies, trailing stop methods, and how to align momentum with price structure. By combining RSI's timing with the trend-following power of moving averages, you now have the tools to build a well-rounded strategy that thrives across multiple market conditions.

Chapter 13: Custom RSI Zones – Breaking Free of 70/30

- Broke the mold of traditional RSI thinking by showing you how to adapt RSI thresholds to better fit different assets, timeframes, and volatility profiles. Instead of relying solely on the classic 70/30 overbought/oversold zones, you learned how custom zones like 80/40 or 60/20 can improve timing, reduce false signals, and match market context. This chapter empowered you to treat RSI like a flexible tool rather than a rigid rulebook, enabling more accurate setups and smarter filters for entries, exits, and confirmations. Now, your RSI strategy can evolve with the market instead of fighting it.

Chapter 14: RSI Automation – Coding RSI Into Your Trading Systems

- Showed you how to automate your RSI-based strategy, reducing emotional interference and increasing consistency. You were introduced to basic scripting, platforms, and logic sequences to build custom systems.

Chapter 15: RSI Psychology – Why It Works and Why It Fails

- made it clear that RSI reflects market psychology—but also your own. You examined how your beliefs, patience, and emotional discipline directly impact how effectively you use RSI.

Chapter 16: The Complete RSI Blueprint – Rules, Filters & Optimization

- Organized all your tools into a structured framework. You developed a repeatable trading plan, filtered out weak signals, and learned how to optimize and backtest your system for continuous improvement.

From Theory to Practice – Applying RSI Live

With all of this under your belt, you're not just a reader anymore—you're a strategist. The next step is applying this knowledge in the real world. Here's how you start:

- **Create a checklist-based system.** Every trade should meet your RSI criteria *and* align with the surrounding context. Example:
    - RSI divergence present?
    - Candlestick confirmation at key level?
    - Multi-timeframe alignment?
    - Favorable volume conditions?

    - Clear exit plan and stop-loss?

- **Use a trading journal.** Document every RSI trade you take. Log:

    - Entry/exit

    - RSI value and signals

    - Supporting confluences

    - Outcome and what you learned

- This builds data-driven confidence, not just emotional hunches.

- **Test and evolve your RSI strategy.** No strategy stays perfect forever. Backtest regularly. Refine based on changing market volatility, risk tolerance, and personal performance.

- **Focus on consistency over perfection.** No RSI strategy will work 100% of the time—but consistency in execution is what separates winning traders from dreamers.

Final Thoughts – From Reading to Results

This book isn't meant to sit on your shelf—it's a roadmap. The traders who succeed with RSI don't just memorize it—they live it. They train their eyes to see opportunities others miss. They develop strategies others ignore. They act with discipline when others chase emotions.

Mastering RSI is not about being right more often—it's about managing risk better, entering more precisely, and trading with confidence backed by logic. You now have the complete blueprint to do exactly that.

You're ready. Start using RSI not just as an indicator—but as a lens through which you see and conquer the market.

Let your RSI knowledge go from concept to capital. From insight to income. From learning... to mastery in motion.

www.ingramcontent.com/pod-product-compliance
Lightning Source LLC
LaVergne TN
LVHW052323200926
848481LV00002B/657
9798868940835